illustrated by
Peter Bellingham

Joanne Bednall

The Greatest
Horse & Pony
Tips in the World

A 'The Greatest in the World' book

www.thegreatestintheworld.com

Illustrations:
Peter Bellingham
www.peterbellinghamillustration.co.uk

Cover & layout design:
the designcouch
www.designcouch.co.uk

Cover images:
© Daniel Guffanti; © Margo Harrison; © Kelly Kane;
© Philippe Minisini; © Beatrice Preve
all courtesy of www.fotolia.com

Copy editor:
Bronwyn Robertson
www.theartsva.com

Series creator/editor:
Steve Brookes

Published in 2007 by
The Greatest in the World Ltd., PO Box 3182
Stratford-upon-Avon, Warwickshire CV37 7XW

Text and illustrations copyright © 2007 – The Greatest in the World Ltd.

All rights reserved. No part of this publication may be reproduced,
stored in a retrieval system, or transmitted in any form or by any means,
electronic, mechanical, photocopying, recording or otherwise, without the
prior permission of the copyright owners. The rights of Joanne Bednall
to be identified as the author of this work has been asserted by
her in accordance with the Copyright, Designs, and Patents Act 1988.
All enquiries regarding any extracts or re-use of any material
in this book should be addressed to the publishers.

A CIP catalogue record for this book is available from the British Library
ISBN 978-1-905151-19-6

Printed and bound in China by 1010 Printing International Ltd.

In memory of
Jean King and Malvern Batchelor.

Contents

Foreword by Jodie Kidd		6
Chapter 1	Horsing around	8
Chapter 2	A stable relationship	28
Chapter 3	A happy horse	44
Chapter 4	Saddle up!	76
Chapter 5	Show time	94
Chapter 6	Tail end	114
Chapter 7	Against the clock	128
Chapter 8	Money matters	144
Index		154
The Greatest in the World books & DVDs		158
The author		160

It is the considered opinion of the author and publisher that the tips contained in this book are the greatest horse & pony tips in the world and are written in good faith. Whilst the author herself is satisfied as to the validity of the tips, neither she nor the publisher will accept any responsibility for any problems that might occur, or any damage or loss sustained due to the use of the information provided herein. This disclaimer has effect only to the extent permitted by English law.

Foreword from Jodie Kidd ...

It is said that horses are a great leveller. They can lift you emotionally when you're feeling down, as well as literally bring you back down to earth if you become over-confident.

In fact, there are few hobbies that can rival the highs and lows of owning, caring for and riding a horse. Whether it's being up to your knees in mud on a cold and dark January morning inspecting the latest ripped rug with frozen fingers, or winning your first rosette at the local show, there's nothing quite like that special bond between horse and rider/owner.

And I should know! Having looked after 30 horses at one stage – not to mention five dogs, four cats and five chickens – I, too, have experienced the rollercoaster ride of emotions that are part and parcel of horse ownership.

For me, nothing beats the exhilaration of galloping along a Caribbean beach or the thrills and spills of playing polo – being a member of Great Britain's winning team at the Women's World Championship was an unforgettable experience.

But equally, just being in the countryside surrounded by horses, mucking them out and getting dirt in my finger nails, is my greatest happiness.

And I've been lucky in that my modelling career has always enabled me to fund my horses – from the showjumpers I competed when I was a teenager to world class polo ponies. Horses always were, and still are – as I currently own a racehorse – my biggest inspiration.

If your bookshelves are anything like mine, heaving under the weight of horsey publications, there will always be room for little books like this one.

Whether you are a seasoned rider or just discovering the wonderful world of horses for the first time, there's something for everyone. From plugging gaps in knowledge – it's ideal for that annual Riding Club quiz – to solving problems while helping you to save time and money, *The Greatest Horse & Pony Tips in the World* is an invaluable addition to every horse lover's library.

Happy riding everyone!

Jodie Kidd

chapter 1
Horsing around

Owning a horse or pony is a huge commitment and responsibility so it's important to ask yourself honestly if you can provide the necessary time, money, experience, knowledge, and facilities. Remember, keeping a horse can sometimes feel like you're ripping up a bunch of tenners every day!

If you've answered yes, yes, yes, yes, and yes, then the next step is to give some careful thought to where the animal will live – most people aren't lucky enough to own a pad in the country with lots of land and stabling. Will you rent a field and shelter or place your horse at livery, thereby passing on the day-to-day responsibility of caring for your horse to someone else? There are aspects to consider before entrusting your horse's care to a professional yard ...

Here are some points to watch out for ...

Do:
- List what's important – whether you want safe off-road riding or an arena to practise your dressage.
- Ensure the yard is run as a business not a hobby or sideline – the former is more likely to treat you as a valued customer.

Don't:
- Opt for a yard where the horses are stabled 24/7.
- Engage the services of inexperienced, unqualified staff.

Living it up

If you opt for livery — where you pay rent to the yard owner on a weekly or monthly basis — decide which arrangement suits your horse and your lifestyle best ...

1. **Grass livery:**
   When the animal lives out. Usually the cheapest arrangement, grass livery is best suited to hardy, native types.

2. **DIY livery:**
   Whereby a field and stable are rented but you do all the work — mucking out, grooming, and feeding.

3. **Part livery:**
   When some of the work is done yourself, usually at weekends, and the rest is carried out by the yard's staff.

4. **Working livery:**
   If you keep your horse at a yard that gives riding lessons, this is quite a good way to keep costs down. Your horse is used in the school as payment towards his keep.

5. **Full livery:**
   The most expensive method. Everything — feed, bedding, grooming — is provided by the yard. All you have to do is turn up and ride! A good arrangement for people who work long hours to pay for their horse and don't have time to undertake stable duties before or after work, although the downside means you have less opportunity to build a relationship together.

Selling points

So you've decided on how and where to keep your horse, what about obtaining one in the first place? Well, you can buy a horse from a private seller, dealer's yard (a good place to find a variety of horses and ponies), or breeder, while auctions, sales and charities are also possible sources but should only be reserved for the very experienced horseperson. When embarking on your equine search mission, never underestimate word of mouth and the local horsey network, such as owners, breeders, instructors, livery yards, and riding schools. If there's a particular horse you like the look of that's not for sale, ask where the owner bought him – if he came from a stud or breeding farm, other horses by the same stallion or out of the same mare might be available.

Search tools

Study the classified section of your local newspapers, Riding Club journal and local and national horse magazines; place wanted ads on the notice boards of local yards, feed merchants, saddlers and riding schools; scour the Internet and flick through your local Yellow Pages or purchase a copy of the British Equestrian Directory for a list of reputable breeders and dealers.

Quick tip

SCAMBUSTERS!
Check the contact details in adverts. If the same phone number crops up time and time again, bear in mind that the seller is probably a dealer – even if stated otherwise.

Points of view

Narrow down a list of possibles to a final shortlist, and call the owners to establish whether the horse will be suitable for your needs after all. Unless experienced in handling and training horses, it's best to avoid a youngster. Be honest about your capabilities and realistic about what you want to achieve.

When arranging a 'test ride', ask the owner if it's OK for you to bring along a knowledgeable friend – ideally, your riding instructor.

10 of the best

When viewing a horse, it makes sense to be organised before you set off so you appear as professional as possible. Remember – most owners won't part with their horse unless they believe he will be 100 per cent happy in his new home.

Here are 10 important questions to take with you to ask the owner:

- Is the horse sound?
- Is he quiet to ride in all respects?
- What has he done previously and would he be suitable for my particular requirements (leisure riding, jumping, etc)?
- Does the horse have any bad habits ('vices' such as weaving, crib biting or windsucking) or failings I should know about, and has he ever bucked, reared, or napped?
- Is he good to catch, box, shoe, and clip?
- Does he hack out happily on his own, in company and in traffic, and has he ever spooked at anything (i.e. tractors, flapping plastic bags)?
- Any previous illnesses/injuries? Is he currently on any medication and why?
- How long have you owned the horse and why is he for sale?
- What's the horse like in the stable and is he OK turned out with both mares and geldings?
- How often is he currently worked and what bit/s and gadget/s is he ridden in?

First impressions

View the horse in a natural light. Does he look well with an alert expression, bright eyes and healthy bloom to his coat?

Check for obvious problems such as evidence of injuries, scars or conformational faults, and run your hands down his legs to feel for any lumps or bumps, which might indicate possible splints or weaknesses. Look for good feet – very important – that are well trimmed and shod with no signs of cracks, and ideally set at an angle of 45 degrees. Shoes should be worn evenly – more wear on the inside or outside, for instance, could indicate a problem with the horse's conformation or way of going.

Ask for the horse to be walked and trotted up and down in hand on a hard surface to check for soundness. Does he move freely and track up?

Quick tip

BEHIND THE SCENES

It's a good idea to see how the horse responds when tacked up, loaded and in his stable, to check he is friendly and has no obvious bad habits. Ensure that he hasn't been denied water – one old trick is to dehydrate a horse to make him quieter and easier to ride.

In the saddle

Not only jump aboard yourself, but ask both the owner and your instructor to ride the horse. That way, you'll be able to see from the ground how the horse moves for both his regular rider and a stranger. Taking along your instructor also means you can ask the unbiased opinion of someone whose knowledge and ability you trust, as well as them acting as a witness should the sale go ahead.

Take your instructor's advice — if he or she suggests that they ride the horse first, then agree, as they are best placed to gauge what the horse is like to ride fresh, and whether he is cold-backed.

Ideally, face the horse with as many different situations as you can: ride him out on his own, in company and in traffic and take him past a few out of the ordinary obstacles or situations, such as a wheelie bin lying on its side, a flapping sheet, some road cones or a tractor, to see how he reacts. Will he go first or last and pass the yard without napping and trying to head for home? If you want him to jump, pop him over a fence or two. Finally, ask yourself if you are:

1. Able to stop the horse?
2. Able to steer him?
3. Happy and comfortable when aboard?

Questions, questions

Don't be afraid to ask seemingly obvious or stupid questions, or to ride the horse again at a different time on another day to get an overall picture.

Find out whether any equipment – such as a saddle, bridle, and rugs – are included in the price, at an extra cost or not at all. Remember that the latter could greatly impact on your budget.

Video star

If trying several horses, ask a friend to video you riding each one so you can review your experiences once you get home, thereby helping you come to a more informed decision.

Decisions, decisions!

Never decide there and then, particularly if you feel under pressure to commit. Go home and think about the horse carefully, making a list of his good and bad points and weighing up the pros and cons.

If you still can't make up your mind, want to see how the horse will react in new or unfamiliar surroundings, or be 100 per cent sure you're making the right decision, ask to have him on a week's trial or for a short loan period. Do get fully insured first, though, as the horse will be your responsibility.

> **Quick tip**
>
> **AVOID LIKE THE PLAGUE...**
> ... a horse that you can't sit on ... can't get on the bit ... scares you ... doesn't respond to your aids. And don't part with your hard-earned cash on the first horse you see!

Comfort zone

Unless very experienced, steer clear of buying a horse with a short neck – these are often very strong to ride, while horses with a long back, upright pasterns, or hocks set out behind can give an uncomfortable ride.

Young at heart

If you've got the time and experience to buy a youngster, look for a good temperament with a nice eye and positive outlook – a generous horse that wants to work.

Other points to look for are a good topline and canter – the latter usually suggests the horse will be easier to train.

In addition, ensure the horse is viceless and you know his history. Look for evidence of bad habits like crib biting, by checking out the condition of the stable and door. If he is on different bedding from the other horses, ask why – he might have an allergy, be prone to lameness/foot problems, or be a box walker.

The write move

Once you have decided to buy, ask for something in writing that confirms the horse is what the vendor says it is. That way, both parties' positions are clear, and should any disputes arise in the future, you'll have some signed evidence to back up your claim.

Deal or no deal?

Your protection under the Sale of Goods Act 1979 is greater if you buy a horse from a dealer, as the sale is classed as a business transaction and means you are entitled to your money back if the horse has a problem that makes him unsuitable for the purpose you bought him.

A good dealer relies on reputation and if the horse has a physical or behavioural problem or does not suit you, they will offer to refund the purchase price or exchange/part-exchange the animal – providing you return him within a certain timeframe. However, don't agree to a dealer taking the horse back only on condition he sells it on for you – you and not the dealer could be sued by the next owner if you fail to disclose a problem.

You are not covered by the above Act at auctions or if you are buying privately – the law 'caveat emptor' (let the buyer beware) exists here, which means you must be able to prove that the vendor knew – or ought to have known – that the horse had a problem, and suing for breach of contract will take time, money, and patience. At the end of the day, it'll be your word against theirs – unless you have something in writing from the seller.

Under the hammer

If you buy from a sale or auction, remember that horses are traditionally sold in guineas (one guinea = £1.05). While some sales deal in pounds, they charge a buyer's premium of 10 per cent of the price (so a £1,200 horse becomes £1,320). If VAT is payable on the sale price, you need to factor that in too.

Sales force

At some sales, the proceeds are taped in case there's any future dispute over what's said. Listen carefully to the information the auctioneer gives out while the horse is in the ring as this might influence your decision on whether or not to bid.

Health check

It goes without saying to always get a horse vetted before finally handing over the cash. Ask an equine vet to carry out a 'five-stage vetting', and tell him or her what activities you want to do with the horse. By asking the horse's current vet to carry out the check, it will mean he is legally obliged to divulge any problems or injuries he may have treated the horse for previously.

A five-stage vetting, done on behalf of the purchaser, comprises:

- A preliminary, stable examination.
- An in-hand examination including trot up, turning and backing.
- A ridden exercise period of 20 minutes at all paces, where possible, so that the horse has performed strenuous exercise.
- A rest period to allow the horse to settle – the time used to further examine/provide identification documentation.
- A final, in-hand trot up and foot examination.

Off to a good start

Congratulations! The horse has passed the vetting and you're on the verge of becoming a fully fledged owner! But in your excitement, don't forget to ask the previous owner:

- The date the horse was last wormed, the brand of wormer used, and the dosage.
- When the horse was last shod and the name of the farrier – if he's in your area.
- What the horse is currently fed, the quantities, brand names, and whether he has any supplements. Is he fed hay or haylage?
- What's his current routine – when is he fed and how long is he turned out for? Try to replicate this as closely as possible until the horse settles into his new home.
- How much exercise he is used to – and whether that's mainly schooling and/or hacking.
- What tack he currently wears, in particular his bit and rugs, depending on the time of year.
- Does the horse have any allergies, perhaps to a certain feedstuff or shampoo? Does he headshake and does he suffer from sweet itch in summer or mud fever in winter?
- Finally, does the horse have any idiosyncracies, quirks or funny habits you should know about – i.e. is he a bit of a Houdini and likes letting himself out of his stable or jumping into the next field, or does he hate having a fly mask put on? Forewarned is forearmed!

Home sweet home

Here are seven ways to introduce your horse to his new surroundings ...

1. Walk him round in-hand, so he gets used to his new home without becoming over-excited.
2. Show him other horses at a distance and then let him settle into his stable for a day or so before turning him out. Youngsters and older horses might find being separated from long-time companions a stressful experience.
3. Placing a piece of familiar equipment into his stable from his previous home, such as an old rug or leadrope, will give him reassurance and comfort. Try softly massaging his ears from the base to the tip to help him relax.
4. Turn your horse out in a field on his own at first, but so he can see and sniff his future field mates over the fence.
5. Once the other horses have accepted him after a few days, turn him out with them under supervision.
6. Wait a week before riding your horse so he's had a chance to settle.
7. The first time you ride him, try to go for a short, relaxing hack in walk so that you can both take in your surroundings and he can get used to the sights and sounds of his new home. Also, this puts no pressure on your horse and shows him that there's nothing to be frightened or wary of – heaping further stress on him is the last thing you want, especially as some horses take a while to settle in to a new routine.

The loan arranger

In many cases, loaning a horse for a set period – say six months – can benefit both the owner and borrower. For instance, the owner might be working abroad or have family commitments, while the borrower might not have the capital to buy a horse, or want a trial period before deciding to splash out permanently.

Get an agreement drawn up including the horse's description (such as any distinguishing marks and freezemark number/identity chip details); owner's and borrower's names and addresses; where the horse is to be kept; whether he has any allergies or special requirements and the notice period (usually a month but an emergency get-out clause could be included to cover mistreatment).

Detail who is responsible for costs, such as farriery and vet's fees; list any equipment – and its condition – that is also loaned out, and state the length of time the agreement is for, who's allowed to ride the horse and what activities can (such as schooling) and can't (such as using the horse for breeding purposes) be undertaken. It is usually down to the lessee to insure the horse at their own expense. Additionally, it's a good idea to include a plan of action if the horse suffers a serious illness or injury and the owner can't be located – can the borrower make the decision to have the horse put down?

You don't need to get a solicitor to draw up the document but copies should be dated and signed by both parties. A sample loan agreement can be downloaded from the British Horse Society (BHS) website.

A fair share

If you don't want the responsibility of owning a horse full-time, then sharing, whereby you contribute towards livery costs and maybe undertake some yard duties, can be the ideal solution. It can benefit the owner, too, as it means the horse is being exercised at times when they perhaps cannot get to the yard. Again, ensure you get an agreement drawn up, and make sure you see the sharer ride your horse in different situations, and that they have the necessary knowledge to groom, tack up, and ride your horse without you supervising.

The borrowers

Leasing is less common but involves the horse being lent to another person for a certain period of time in return for payment. Competition or stud horses are sometimes leased.

Which breed is best?

There are more than 150 – perhaps as many as 200 – equine breeds in the world today, so deciding which one is right for you can be a real horsey headache. Here are my 10 favourite breeds (in alphabetical order!) ...

1. **Andalusian**
   This noble breed's agility, balance, action and paces mean it's ideal for High School dressage and as the chosen mount of the Spanish 'rejoneador' (bullfighter).

2. **Arab**
   Its powers of endurance and stamina make this showy breed virtually unbeatable at long-distance riding events all over the world. Forward-going, Arabs and part-Arabs are usually agile and can turn their hoof to most equestrian disciplines, although rarely excel at top-level dressage because of their body shape.

3. **Connemara**
   Ireland's pony star, the Connemara is courageous, fast, sensible, and hardy. The breed excels at showjumping, dressage and showing – especially when crossed with the Thoroughbred. Such are its qualities that 'oversize' Connemaras of 15hh and more are now becoming popular.

4. **Dutch Warmblood**
   Holland's leading competition horse has produced some of the world's star equine performers in showjumping, dressage, and carriage driving.

5. **Hanoverian**
   A German warmblood, the Hanoverian has earned an international reputation as a top-class showjumper and dressage horse.

6. **Irish Draught**
   When crossed with the Thoroughbred to create the Irish Hunter, this athletic former farm horse is a world-beater across country.

7. **Quarter Horse**
   Arguably America's most versatile breed, the Quarter Horse is the fastest equine in the world over a quarter of a mile. It's popular for rodeos, racing, ranch work, and trail riding.

8. **Shetland**
   This pint-size pony is the strongest in the world relative to its size. Formerly used as a pack animal, the Shetland is popular today in harness, as a children's riding pony, and as a field companion.

9. **Shire**
   This gentle giant, often weighing more than one tonne, was Britain's main source of pre-war industrial and agricultural power. Numbers dwindled rapidly during the 20th century but working museums and brewery companies have helped revive the breed.

10. **Thoroughbred**
    Universally acknowledged as the fastest — and most valuable — breed in the world. Thoroughbreds tend to be sensitive, energetic, intelligent and agile — qualities needed in a good eventer. Not very hardy, though, Thoroughbreds don't tend to winter out well.

Honesty is the best policy

Definitely the best advice when selling a horse. If you are truthful about the horse and his abilities, you won't have to refund any money; but the buyer can take legal action against you if you fail to disclose any problem.

Don't be tempted to over-inflate the horse's ability in order to impress potential purchasers — stick to the facts, not your opinion as to what the horse might or might not achieve in the future.

Don't fall into the trap of over-inflating a horse's price either, just because you or someone else believes he has potential. If you think the horse could compete at Grand Prix dressage in the future but hasn't yet tackled an unaffiliated prelim test, prospective purchasers aren't likely to gamble and pay over the odds — especially if the horse's breeding isn't up to scratch. Look at classified adverts in the 'horses for sale' section of the equestrian press or on the Internet and set the price according to horses of a similar height, age, breeding and achievements thus far.

> ## Quick tip
>
> **TAKING TURNS**
> If you are leading your horse to show to a vet or potential purchaser, remember to turn him away from you so he doesn't tread on your toes and you don't obscure their view.

Rules is rules

When prospective purchasers test ride your horse, ensure they are wearing the right gear – proper riding boots and an up-to-standard hat – or you could be held negligent if there's an accident.

Also check that they are insured to ride your horse, either through your own cover or theirs.

If someone asks to have your horse for a trial period, first draw up a written agreement as to who's responsible for what and insist that they are insured.

It might suit you to sell your horse through a dealer – in which case, make sure you agree their percentage in advance (usually around 10 per cent). And check whether you will be liable for any livery, farriery, or other costs while the horse is between owners. Ask the dealer to sign a document setting out what's been agreed.

Peace of mind

Once you have accepted an offer, draw up a sales agreement, detailing the horse's age, breed, height, and past achievements. If the horse has no vices, ask the buyer to sign a statement saying that you have disclosed this to them.

And ask a friend or relative to act as a witness to corroborate your conversation with the buyer.

If the sale subsequently goes sour, don't be bullied into giving the buyer their money back if they say the horse isn't what they wanted after all – that's not a good enough reason!

chapter 2
A stable relationship

Horses are herd animals and prefer living outside in their natural surroundings to being in a stable all the time. If your horse is stabled as part of his daily routine, or he is on box rest following an injury, there are various measures you can adopt to tackle boredom and reduce the risk of him developing bad habits.

Boredom breakers

Try to ensure your horse has a clear view of the yard's activities or he can see, or is close to, an equine pal. Alternatively, swap stables so he gets a different view.

It's possible to buy haynets with smaller holes (for haylage) – or placing a haynet inside another haynet will have the same effect – which will take your horse longer to chomp through his daily ration.

Digging deep

Mucking out is the core duty of any stable management routine. Soiled bedding should be removed from the stable at least twice a day, otherwise leaving a horse standing on it for long periods can lead to him developing breathing and hoof problems – specifically thrush, an unpleasant foot disease.

Brain teasers

There is a vast array of stable toys on the market, including balls that let out a small amount of food at a time, keeping even the most laid-back of horses occupied for hours. If your horse doesn't show much interest at first, hang up the toy by its handle and smear a small amount of treacle on it.

Alternatively, making your own toy by suspending a turnip or swede on a strand of baler twine from the roof or tying a plastic squeezey bottle of peppermint-flavoured water to the bars or from the roof, not only gives hours of amusement but also encourages mental agility.

Leaving a whole swede on his stable floor for your horse to nibble at is another natural, safe method of 'home entertainment'!

One old tip is to cut bunches of gorse (with gloved hands!) and tie the stalks together, hanging them upside down in his stable. It's said that horses enjoy mouthing the prickly stems.

In addition, to beat boredom, take your horse out for short walks in-hand, perhaps allowing him to graze for 15 minutes, and leave the radio on – rumour has it that horses prefer classical music!

Remember – even turning your horse out in an enclosed area, such as a sand arena or indoor school for half an hour, is better than no turnout at all.

And finally, even chickens and ducks can be good company for a lonely horse!

Door to door

If your horse crib bites while in his stable, deter him by smearing mustard on the top of the door or fit a grille or metal plate/length of tough plastic drainpipe over the stable door.

For horses which scrape the floor in front of their stable door with a forefoot, put a rubber mat there to prevent shoes getting worn and to stop the noise. Similarly, a piece of old carpet or a sack stuffed with straw nailed to the inside of the bottom door will muffle the noise if your horse tends to kick it, especially at feed time.

And if your horse is a barger, fixing a breast bar across the inside of the doorway can remedy this. It's also a good way of keeping the stable cool in summer.

Quick tip

A CUT ABOVE

No knife or scissors to hand? To cut that annoying twine on straw and hay bales, the best solution is, well, another length of baler twine! Use it in a sawing motion to fray the twine you want to remove.

Remember to place all pieces of baler twine in a separate bag so it doesn't get mixed up in bedding or a haynet.

Which bed is best?

A deep, clean bed keeps a horse warm, encourages him to lie down and soaks up soiling.

Never allow your horse to stand on a bare floor as he will splash his legs when relieving himself, which will discourage him from staling altogether.

The most popular types of bedding are straw (wheat is best as horses are more likely to eat oat straw), wood shavings (better for horses with an allergy), shredded paper and rubber matting (increasing in popularity as owners are recognising the long-term cost savings).

If your horse has respiratory problems or tends to eat a straw bed, and shavings are too costly, then how about using cardboard or wood fibre/pulp as an alternative? For owners who prefer to muck out daily than skip out a deep litter bed, baled, chopped cardboard is ideal as it is clean, low in dust, highly absorbent and very insulating.

Dried, shredded, wood fibre bedding, on the other hand, provides a warm, comfortable bed and offers low dust levels and excellent absorbency and drainage — perfect if your horse suffers from foot conditions such as thrush. Dried wood pulp is similar in terms of dust and absorbency levels and can also be deep littered or skipped out daily plus it's recyclable and 'green'.

Forking out

When buying a set of yard tools, remember to include a:

- Four-tined fork to muck out straw beds or a shavings fork for, well, shavings.
- Broom – brushes with bahia, a natural fibre rather than nylon, are best.
- Wheelbarrow.
- Shovel.
- Pair of rubber gloves to capture those annoying stray droppings.
- Yard knife with a concealed blade for cutting through baler twine and slitting open feed and shavings bags.
- Skep or muck basket for fields.

Don't muck about!

If your muck heap is becoming more of a mountain than a molehill, then the time has come to reduce this growing blot on your landscape.

Ask your local farmer if he can use the muck as fertiliser on his fields (but not on grazing land due to the risk of worm infestation) in return for taking it away himself. Otherwise an agricultural contractor or removal specialist will remove the muck for a charge (look in your local Yellow Pages or the advertising section of the equine press, or the Internet). Ensure that a tractor has easy access to your muck heap before calling anyone out.

A stable relationship

> The essential joy of being with horses is that it brings us in contact with the rare elements of grace, beauty, spirit, and fire.

Sharon Ralls Lemon

Muck in!

Keep future muck at a manageable level by advertising it to local gardeners via a sign on the road, in your local newspaper/parish magazine, or on the notice board at local garden centres and nurseries.

Get everyone at the yard to lend a hand to bag it up — although some gardeners prefer to collect it themselves straight from the field.

Stable minds

Before building timber stables, first check whether you need planning permission. You may not need approval if you are replacing existing stables or erecting stables in your garden, but run it by your local council's planning department first. Unless you've built a stable before, it's best to contact specialist contractors for quotes rather than risk a potential DIY nightmare!

First foundations

When building stables, 15 cm (6") of hardcore should be put down before laying a concrete base 10 cm (4") deep. A special equine mix of concrete should be used as horse's urine is acidic and can corrode ordinary concrete. The base should slope, enabling urine to drain away, while the stables must have adequate drainage and ventilation. Ideally, they shouldn't face north or be situated close to trees with far-reaching roots. All stables should have strong timber kickboards extending to at least half the height of the walls.

Getting the brush off

Grooming keeps horses clean and healthy by removing dirt and sweat from their coats, and helps to keep their pores open. It also encourages the blood to circulate and promotes muscle and skin tone, thereby improving the horse's overall condition and appearance.

Also, grooming helps prevent disease and lessens the risk of sores and skin problems developing.

Every well-formed, self-respecting grooming kit should be bursting at the seams with the following items:

- **Body brush** – to clean the horse's body and mane and tail.
- **Dandy brush** – its stiff bristles are excellent for removing dried mud on legs.
- **Water brush** – for dampening and laying the mane and tail.
- **Hoof pick** – used in a heel to toe motion to remove mud and stones from your horse's feet.
- **Metal, rubber and/or plastic curry comb** – the former is solely for cleaning brushes, while the latter two can be used on the horse's body to remove dried mud and loose hairs from the coat.
- **Sweat scraper** – for removing excess water and sweat from the coat following a bath or energetic workout.
- **At least two sponges** – for cleaning the nostrils and eyes and the dock area: baby wipes are good to use on the nose and dock, as they have cleansing and moisturising properties but don't use them around the eyes or on any broken skin.

- **Stable rubber** although an old tea towel is just as good — for removing dust and giving the coat a final polish.
- **Mane comb** — for combing the mane prior to plaiting.
- **Hoof oil and brush**, however pure vegetable oil (or mixing a little Stockholm tar with vegetable cooking oil) can be just as effective — for replacing some of the natural oil in your horse's feet lost by wet, muddy conditions, and for adding a finishing touch to your horse's appearance.

Grooming dos and don'ts:

Do:

- Use a rubber curry comb in a circular motion to remove a horse's winter coat as the new summer coat starts to grow through.

- Buy two different coloured sponges and delegate which colour is to be used for your horse's dock area and which one for the eyes and nostrils – and stick to it.

- Use a small amount of baby oil in water to get rid of dust from your horse's coat, particularly if he's been clipped. Simply wipe over with a wrung out tea towel. Baby wipes are great for this too!

- Put a few drops of baby oil on a soft brush and brush through a clean tail to prevent tangles and stop the hair becoming brittle. It helps prevent white hairs getting discoloured, too.

- Hold your horse's tail firmly to one side with your spare hand if he's ticklish and you're grooming round the hindquarters. That way, he's less likely to kick out and you'll feel his tail twitching as an early warning sign if he's cross.

- Clean your grooming kit at the same time as you bath your horse – otherwise you'll brush dirt straight back into his coat.

Don't:

- Use a dandy brush or plastic curry comb on your horse's mane and tail, as this can cause the hairs to split and break.
- Over-groom a grass-kept horse in winter as this removes the natural grease in his coat, which he needs for protection from the elements. Basic grooming with a dandy brush to get rid of dried mud (not a body brush as its short close-set hairs are designed to really get into a horse's coat to remove dirt and grease), and picking the feet out daily will suffice (excrement is full of ammonia, which will attack the hoof if it's not cleaned out regularly).
- Clip legs as the hair allows water to drain off the ergot and not into the heel, thereby reducing the risk of winter ailments such as cracked heels and mud fever. Leaving the mane and tail full provides extra warmth.

Quick tip

AND REMEMBER...

... if grooming your horse outside his stable, always tie him – using a quick release knot – to breakable string attached to a metal ring. This means that should he pull back, the string, rather than the horse's headcollar or fence post, will break first and is less likely to cause injury.

A good pick-me-up!

There's nothing more annoying than losing — or someone borrowing and not returning — tools from your grooming kit. Hoofpicks are one of the most likely items to go AWOL, as everyone needs one and they're so easy to misplace.

How about attaching a length of colourful baler twine to your hoofpick so that (a) it's easier to spot when dropped in your horse's bedding, (b) you can instantly identify it as yours, and (c) it can be hung on a nail in the tack room so that you don't have to go scrabbling around for it in the bottom of your grooming box.

Safe not sorry

In today's world, horseowners are no different from any other section of society when it comes to protecting gear, property, transport, and even your horse from vandals and thieves. Here are a few ways of stepping up security at your yard ...

Guard that gear!

To prevent your gear being stolen or 'permanently borrowed', write your or your horse's name in indelible felt pen on the inside/underside of nylon girths, headcollars, and numnahs. Alternatively, sew on name tapes.

Secure your saddle with one of the many different types of saddle lock on the market, and/or ask your local crime prevention officer to stamp leather and wooden items with your postcode.

Be horse smart

Vary the time of day you visit your horse if you can so your movements aren't predicted by a thief.

Have your horse freezemarked, identity chipped, or your postcode branded onto his hooves – although the latter method will need repeating as the horn grows downwards. Opportunist thieves especially are less likely to steal a horse with an obvious mark that's easily traced. Plus, reputable sales and abattoirs are equipped with scanners to check for identity chips.

Ideally, turn your horse out without his headcollar – unless he's difficult to catch – to make life harder for thieves.

Do you keep your horse at home? If you have enough land (and no neighbours!) consider installing the best alarm system in the world – a gaggle of geese!

If your horse is stolen, inform the police and Horsewatch's Stolen Horse Register as soon as possible. Circulate a poster with his photograph and details to local riding schools, tack shops, livery yards, training establishments, studs, feed merchants, vets, sales/auctions, and abattoirs.

For horses that are freezemarked, phone the company, which will circulate your animal's details to sales and slaughterhouses. Also ring your insurance company – they might help you with recovery expenses – and call or text as many horsey friends as possible to alert them to the fact that thieves are operating in the area.

A stable relationship

Property protection

If budget allows, fit an intruder alarm at the yard and consider installing closed circuit TV.

Security lights that come on automatically when they detect movement are a worthwhile investment.

Ensure your tack room door/s are padlocked and have metal bars or a grille fitted to any windows or skylights.

Put up visible notices on the yard and gates warning that all horses and tack are security marked.

Make sure a padlock and chain are fitted to BOTH ends of gates so that they can't be lifted off their hinges. Alternatively, reverse the top hinge or weld metal plates over the hinges.

Lock that lorry!

Remember to secure your lorry or trailer too — both at home and at shows. Lock all doors and ensure the ramp is up. Try to park it in a well-lit area, as close to other vehicles as possible. Wheel clamps, hitchlocks, lock down devices, and installing a Tracker are all excellent ways of deterring thieves.

Mark the vehicle inside and out with your postcode, including the spare wheel, breast bars, and partitions.

Postcoding the trailer's roof with large letters/numbers in a contrasting colour is an excellent way to both guard against theft and recover the vehicle if it is ever stolen, as it can be instantly spotted from the air by any passing police helicopter or Sky Watch volunteer pilot. The wide tape used for silage sacks is ideal for this.

Snap decision

Photograph everything – your horse, tack, and trailer/lorry – just in case any of your possessions are stolen. Take a hair sample from your horse as this might provide definitive identification, and record the serial numbers of all items of equipment.

Be a nosy neighbour

It makes sense to build good relations with any neighbours, and encourage them to stay vigilant too. Find out the name and contact details of your area Horsewatch co-ordinator, and find out the names of your local police officer and Neighbourhood Watch co-ordinator – as well as the best way to get hold of them.

Stay alert

Finally, if you see a strange vehicle parked near your yard or field, note down the registration number, make of car and time you saw it. A favourite trick for thieves is to park some distance away and lead a horse back to their vehicle. Keep a close eye on trailers or lorries parked in lay-bys or gateways. Be particularly suspicious if you see anyone video recording horses or property as many thieves operate on a 'steal to order' basis.

Check hedges and gates regularly as holes made in the former and bolts and hinges loosened on the latter will often be done in advance to clear exits and hasten departure.

And watch for anything out of the ordinary such as the yard dog sleeping more than usual (he could have been doped).

chapter 3

chapter 3
A happy horse

Ensuring that your horse is fed a suitable diet, as well as paying close attention to his worming programme, teeth, and feet, are all part and parcel of responsible horse ownership.

Cut out chopping!

Horses love succulents, such as apples and carrots, as treats or part of their daily diet. When adding these to your horse's feed, ALWAYS slice them lengthways into 'fingers' and NEVER chop them. Otherwise you risk pieces lodging in your horse's throat, causing him to choke.

Oil's well ...

Cod liver oil is not only a highly palatable supplement to your horse's diet but it improves bone integrity for healthy joints and helps promote general wellbeing.

Get up and go!

If you feel your horse needs an extra energy boost, perhaps at a show, then give him a banana – minus the skin, of course! The fruit is an excellent source of potassium, needed by nerves and muscles to function effectively.

It's said that a double handful of glucose or a bottle of stout added to a mash or feed can be a good pick-me-up too!

Grub's up!

The 10 golden rules of equine feeding are:

- Feed little and often – horses have sensitive and relatively small stomachs.
- Provide a constant supply of clean, fresh water – change regularly as it absorbs ammonia from the stable atmosphere and becomes unpleasant to drink.
- Feed plenty of good quality hay, especially in winter when grass has little nutritional value.
- Add succulents (i.e. apples or carrots) to meals.
- Feed according to your horse's size, temperament, and workload.
- Introduce any changes to your horse's diet gradually so as not to upset his stomach.
- Never exercise your horse less than an hour and a half after feeding him.
- Keep feeding utensils – such as buckets, bowls, and scoops – spotlessly clean.
- Keep food in rat resistant metal or plastic bins with the lids on firmly.
- Ensure meal times are regular – horses prefer routine.

Quick tip

TYRED OUT

Does your horse tend to kick over his bucket at feed time? Then put an end to that trick by placing it inside an old tyre.

Fast food!

With horses who bolt their food, try …

… splitting it into three or four small feeds a day;

… putting his feed into a corner manger, which has a larger surface area;

… feeding off the floor and spread it around so he can't take large mouthfuls at once;

… putting chaff into hard feed so he has to chew for longer;

… placing a large rounded stone or salt lick/lump of rock salt in the manger so he has to eat around it.

Take care!

Make sure you tie your horse's haynet at the right height – too high and he'll have to stretch up unnaturally for his hay; too low and he might get his feet caught in it.

If you use buckets on the stable floor instead of an automatic water system, it might be safer to remove the handles (and bring the hose to the bucket rather than the other way around!) so your horse can't get caught up or injure himself.

A happy horse

Slowly does it

Is your horse a fussy eater? Encourage him to eat by washing your hands before mixing his feed, as horses can be put off their food by unpleasant smells.

Mix a couple of tablespoons of nutritious and palatable honey in to his feed to make it that bit more appetising. Alternatively, try adding molasses or black treacle (dilute with five parts warm water and sprinkle from a watering can over hay) to sweeten his food. Ensure you are giving sweet-smelling hay – soft calf hay is better than hard seed hay. If your horse prefers damp hay to dry hay, consider feeding haylage – which can be sweeter and more palatable than hay.

Make sure the concentrates you buy are fresh by checking the manufacturing rather than 'best before' date (some companies place a three-month shelf life on their feed while others are four months or more). Feed that's past its sell-by date will certainly not go down well with fussy eaters!

Find out what texture of feed your horse prefers – damp, wet, dry, mashed, or a combination – and study the ingredients – cubes or mixes? Some alfalfa or grass cubes in low-energy foods can be sour or bitter. Providing succulents such as apples and carrots will add variety and interest.

Winter warmers

If your horse starts to lose weight in winter, try adding extra oil to his diet, in the form of soya, corn, or sunflower oil. For older horses with loose or missing teeth, help maintain their weight by feeding high fibre cubes (or conditioning cubes if there are several missing teeth) as a partial or total hay replacer, soaked into a mash with water or sugar beet pulp.

Sugar beet is commonly fed during winter as it has good energy and fibre levels, is a good succulent, provides liquid in the diet, tempts fussy eaters, and can be added to chaff, mixes or cubes to prevent the feed becoming sloppy. But remember to **ALWAYS** soak sugar beet in cold water for 12 hours (shreds) or 24 hours (pellets) prior to feeding, as unsoaked it will swell in the horse's sensitive gut and could prove fatal.

If kept more than 24 hours, particularly in hot weather, sugar beet is also prone to ferment – throw it away if it smells sweet and has turned light brown as this could cause colic.

Feeding linseed is another way to add both weight and condition – it's easily digestible and can give your horse's coat a healthy bloom. Prepare a jelly by using 20 parts of water to one of linseed and soak for six hours. Strain off the water and replace it with fresh water. Bring it to the boil in a saucepan and simmer uncovered for four hours, stirring occasionally. Feed a teacupful two or three times a week – but check that the seeds have broken first. **NEVER** feed uncooked linseed as the raw seeds are poisonous.

Breathe easy

If your horse has a respiratory disorder – often exacerbated by dusty stables, indoor schools, and bedding – you might find his condition improves if he's fed good quality haylage, but introduce it gradually so as not to upset his gut. If used within three to five days of opening, haylage has a higher nutritional value and lower dust content than hay, and has a water content of around 35 to 50 per cent, while hay has 15 per cent.

Feeding a garlic supplement, with its expectorant and antibiotic properties, can also benefit horses with mild respiratory problems, such as a runny nose, wheezing, or coughing. Garlic also boosts skin condition and the immune system as well as being an effective fly repellent.

Plant power

Provided they are fed under an homeopathic vet's guidance, herbs can balance deficiencies in your horse's diet. Here are three useful herbs:

1. **Stinging nettle:** Rich in vitamin C, iron, sodium, chlorophyll, protein and dietary fibre, can ward off sweet itch and help circulation – useful for laminitis, rheumatism and arthritis.

2. **Comfrey:** Reputed to heal bone damage such as sore shins, chipped knees, stress fractures and arthritis, as well as tendon strains. Said to soothe respiratory conditions.

3. **Dandelion:** A good source of potassium, calcium, iron and beta carotene, can aid kidney and liver complaints, stimulate appetite and boost digestion. Useful for rheumatism, arthritis and laminitis.

In good health

A healthy horse will have salmon pink-coloured gums, nostrils, and third eyelid. Press his gums with your finger – it should take no more than a couple of seconds for the area to return to its normal colour.

Get to know what's normal for your horse and become familiar with the shape of his legs so you're more likely to spot any lumps, bumps, and swellings as soon as they occur. Check your horse's legs carefully when you bring him in from the field, as this could make the difference between a sound horse and one with a big infected leg that can rapidly develop when a small wound is missed.

Take your horse's respiration, heart rate and temperature regularly (once in summer and again in winter) and record the results so you know what's normal for him.

Too hot to handle?

The normal temperature for an adult horse is 37–38°C (100–101°F). Take his temperature by greasing the measuring end of a special veterinary thermometer with saliva or petroleum jelly – an easy-to-read digital one is best (although a human glass thermometer will work too, provided you shake the mercury to the bottom of the scale first). Insert it 4cm (1½") into the horse's anus for one minute, ensuring it tilts against the wall of the rectum. Then remove and wipe the thermometer with cotton wool or a tissue and read it before thoroughly cleaning with cold water and disinfectant. Call the vet if your horse's temperature goes above 40°C (102.5°F).

A happy horse

Keep the beat

Find your horse's heartbeat on the left side of his lower chest, just behind the elbow where the girth would go. Remember that a horse's heart rate at rest varies with breed, age, and fitness.

It's easier to find your horse's pulse after he has been working when it is stronger and more obvious. Feel for it on the mandibular artery, under the jaw bone; inside the foreleg just below the elbow; either side of the back of the fetlock or either side of the tail under the dock. Use the flat of your first three fingers and count the number of beats in 15 seconds before multiplying by four to get the pulse rate per minute. The resting heart rate of a healthy adult horse is usually between 30 and 42 beats per minute, but can increase to 200 beats per minute during strenuous exercise.

At competitions, cold water, applied liberally all over your horse – especially to his quarters, which produce the most heat – will help bring down his pulse.

Take a breather

Your horse's respiration rate at rest should be 8–12 breaths per minute – watch the walls of his abdomen or chest wall move as each breath is taken.

> It's a lot like
> nuts and bolts …
> If the rider's nuts,
> the horse bolts.

The Horse Whisperer

A helping hand

You or your yard should have a first aid kit, stored in a waterproof box, within easy reach in the tack room in case of emergencies. It should include:

- Cotton wool for cleaning wounds but not as a dressing.
- Gamgee to cushion and protect injuries.
- A well-stocked supply of dressings, including Animalintex, an all purpose veterinary poultice and dressing.
- A variety of flexible cohesive bandages to keep dressings in place and provide protection.
- Elastoplast to use as an adhesive bandage, particularly for difficult areas like around the knee and hock.
- A large animal thermometer for taking your horse's temperature – the digital ones are not only accurate but good if the light is poor.
- Blunt ended scissors for trimming hair from wounds.
- Waterproof medical tape for holding bandages or dressings in place.
- Wound gel to help combat infection and speed up the healing process.
- Salt for making saline solution – NEVER use Dettol.
- A conforming (gauze) bandage.
- A cold pack to reduce inflammation and heat.
- Tissues.
- Antiseptic wash.
- Soap.

- Exercise/tail bandages.
- 50ml syringe.
- Vaseline.
- Tweezers.
- Small torch.
- Pen and paper.

Wound warnings

Horses are always picking up cuts and scrapes in the field or stable, and it's important to treat even the most minor abrasion. Always follow the 'Three C Rule', whether the injury is a small cut, puncture wound, or major laceration: clean, clot, and cover.

Wash your hands thoroughly in antiseptic solution before touching any wound. First, gently hose the area with cold water to cleanse the wound, wash away the blood, and reveal the wound site. Treat the area – usually on the horse's leg – with a wound gel (it might help afterwards to trim the hair from the edges to guard against contamination). Then use a sterile non-adherent dressing to hold the wound gel in place, wrap a layer of cotton wool or Gamgee around the leg followed by a stretch bandage, and finally something such as Vetrap to hold it in place. If a wound is bleeding profusely, try to stop the flow before calling the vet.

Also call the vet if:

- Your horse is lame (even if the wound looks innocent).
- The wound is more than two inches long and has gone right through the skin.
- There's a foreign body, such as a stake or piece of metal, embedded in the skin.
- If your horse hasn't had an anti-tetanus vaccination.
- You suspect a vital structure – such as a joint – might be involved.
- The wound is located near or directly over joints or tendons.

- A yellowy-coloured liquid (joint fluid) is leaking from the wound.
- There is a continuous stream or spurt of blood. Blood from a vein is much darker – maybe even brown – and will ooze rather than gush from a wound as it is flowing back to the heart. A venous injury is less serious than an arterial one, which is much brighter in colour, often appearing orange and can spurt as far as seven or eight feet. The average horse has around 50 pints of blood and can lose five pints without it being life-threatening.

Hot spot

On a hot day, especially if you have been working your horse or competing, watch that he doesn't become dehydrated. Pinch a fold of his skin and if it 'tents' – remains pinched and doesn't spring back to its normal position – then he's dehydrated. Look also for sunken eyes, dry, tacky mucus membranes, and reduced urine output. Offer plenty of water, as well as electrolytes, but don't allow grass or concentrates – hay is OK though.

Some competition horses might benefit from an iron supplement in summer to guard against anaemia – but check with your vet first.

In recovery

If your horse tries to take off a bandage with his teeth, use a bib or muzzle or paint the outside of the bandage with a foul-tasting substance.

With a leg injury, bandage the horse's opposite limb as well for support, especially if he's lame and bearing most of his weight on to his good leg.

Once a superficial graze has healed over, rub in some petroleum jelly as this will keep the area supple and help prevent the newly healed area from cracking open again.

Remember that wounds heal from side to side, not end to end, so even what looks like a big hole that will never close up, will heal well.

Witch-hazel can be applied externally to any bruised areas and can be added to water when washing down a horse's legs.

Nappies make good foot dressings as they are easy to fit, stay on well, and are extremely waterproof!

You can disguise the taste of your horse's medicine by using molasses in his feed, hiding it inside an apple, carrot, or slice of bread, or mixing it with black treacle and smearing it on his tongue with a wooden spoon.

Breath of fresh air

If your horse has a dust allergy and coughs (an ailment called RAO – Recurrent Airway Obstruction – formerly known as COPD), there are ways to combat this ...

- Feed good quality dust-free hay or haylage or soak your hay for 20 minutes to wash out or swell any mould spores, which will reduce coughing.
- Turn your horse out as much as possible so exposure to dust and mould spores in his stable is kept to a minimum.
- Ensure his stable has good ventilation.
- Muck out while your horse is turned out, to reduce dust levels.
- Groom your horse outside.
- Store hay and straw as far away from his stable as possible.
- Use dust-free or low-dust bedding – rubber matting is the best solution.
- For severe cases, brondhodilators (to reverse airway spasm, eg. Ventipulmin TM), mucolytics (to help clear mucus from the lungs, eg. Sputolosin TM) and corticosteroids (to reduce airway inflammation) can be used.

The latter can be extremely effective, but have undesirable side-effects when used in the long term.

Inhalation therapy – using metered dose inhalers similar to those used by human asthma sufferers – can also help. A plastic 'baby haler' spacer is fitted over one nostril while the other is kept closed.

A happy horse

Mud – not so glorious – mud

Mud fever is a common winter ailment, caused by bacteria that affect the heel, pastern and fetlock, resulting in scabs and sores.

With horses prone to the condition – particularly greys and those with white legs – prevention is better than cure. If yours is susceptible, try to limit his exposure to muddy areas – although this is often easier said than done.

Bring in your horse regularly from the field to allow the mud to dry and be removed. Alternatively, hose the mud off his legs with cold water – warm water will open the pores and encourage bacterial infection to enter the skin – before drying thoroughly and applying first a barrier ointment then breathable bandages or stable bandages over Gamgee.

Affected horses should have their legs washed daily with a mild antibacterial or homeopathic shampoo and the scabs removed.

In milder cases, ensure affected areas are clean and dry before applying Vaseline and grease to your horse's heels. This will act as a barrier against wet and muddy conditions.

For horses that suffer badly from the condition, try cleaning and drying their legs before applying a good layer of antibacterial cream and then wrapping the affected areas in cling film with Gamgee and a stable bandage on top. This causes the legs to sweat, making the scabs softer and easier to remove. But remember to change the dressing once a day.

If the condition becomes serious, stable your horse and seek veterinary advice, which may include treatment with antibiotics.

Slippery customers

Devising a thorough worming programme for your horse ensures his internal organs don't become a parasites' playground!

Change wormers (not just the brand but check the ingredients on the label for a different anthelmintic) every year, but not every time so the little devils don't build up a resistance to a certain product, and worm all horses on the yard at once. Worm all new arrivals and keep them stabled for 48 hours afterwards so that they don't contaminate the pasture.

In December, give your horse a single dose of Ivermectin to cut short the cycle of the bot fly, which lays its characteristic yellow eggs on horses' legs in the summer.

Place worm powders in the fridge a day or so before giving to your horse as this helps reduce the smell and makes them more palatable.

Teeth trouble

If your horse eats very carefully or takes longer to eat than normal; there's a lot of undigested food in his droppings; he 'quids' (drops food out of his mouth) or there's any strong smell from his mouth, then it's time to call an equine dentist.

Don't ride your horse – or use a hackamore (bitless bridle) until the dentist has been – it could just be his teeth need rasping to file down any sharp edges.

It makes sense for your horse to have an annual dental check up as painful teeth might explain various riding and/or behavioural problems.

A happy horse

Feet first

The phrase 'no foot, no horse' has never been more true. Horses need new shoes every six to eight weeks – or even less if you ride a lot on the roads. But even if your horse is unshod, he should still have his feet trimmed regularly by a qualified farrier.

If you find your horse is suffering from crumbling or splitting hooves and can't keep shoes on, try putting an egg in his feed every day – you should find the new growth is far stronger thanks to the extra protein. Alternatively, for a similar effect, rub in mutton fat from the Sunday lunch or local butcher, or add a sachet of gelatine dissolved in a mugful of hot water to a feed each day.

Does your horse tend to trip or stumble – perhaps because he's getting on in years? Then ask your farrier about fitting rolled toes on the front shoes, and possibly the hind ones too. This will enable your horse to roll his foot off the ground rather than having to lift it uncomfortably high.

For riders who are restricted to hacking mainly on the roads, and find their horses tend to slip on the Tarmac surface, ask a farrier to fit a road nail (or pair of road studs if extra grip is needed) into each shoe.

A splashing time

For those of us lucky enough to live near the sea or a safe-flowing river – or even an equine swimming pool – it's worth taking the plunge and introducing your horse to water therapy for the following reasons ...

- To vary routine – swimming is excellent for sweetening up bored or sour horses, particularly those on box rest following an injury.
- Following certain operations, particularly knee or fetlock arthroscopies.
- For laminitics, because swimming keeps the weight off their feet.
- For horses with tendon and ligament strains and foot problems such as bruised feet.
- To help reduce general bruising, stiffness and soreness.
- For horses with bad backs.
- As part of your exercise or fittening routine, particularly if the ground is too wet in winter or too hard during the summer, or due to frost. Endurance horses, trotters, hunters, racehorses, point-to-pointers, eventers, showjumpers, show ponies, and police horses have all benefited from horsey hydrotherapy.

An easy catch

So you can't catch your horse? A common problem, this one. Nothing is more annoying than being unable to get your horse in from the field, especially when the weather is foul or you're in a hurry.

In a herd situation, horses develop certain roles like lookouts, followers, and leaders. Establish which horse yours prefers to follow, and bring him in first. Often, once all the other horses have been caught, even the most wilful might decide it's best to come in after all.

Other tricks like rustling a crisp packet, hiding the headcollar and rattling a few nuts or stones in a bucket can sometimes make all the difference.

Walking confidently up to a horse's shoulder and making slow, deliberate movements so as not to startle him, might help too.

Quick tip

TURNING THE TABLES
When turning your horse out, don't allow him to gallop off into the distance, spraying you with dirt and mud. Instead, turn him calmly to face the gate before taking off his headcollar. That way you're less likely to get kicked.

Having a field day

Patrol your paddock on a regular basis to ensure it remains a safe haven for your horse. As well as keeping the level of droppings to a minimum, pick up any rubbish, fill in rabbit holes/tramp down molehills, mend broken fencing, remove protruding nails, and pull up and burn any poisonous plants (see p66). Nail broken rails on to your horse's side of the post – this will make it more difficult for him to push them off in the future by leaning or rubbing against the fence.

Watch out for anyone throwing garden rubbish such as grass cuttings or hedge clippings into your horse's field – remove immediately as this can cause colic if eaten.

When feeding hay in the field, always put out one pile more than the number of horses to prevent squabbling.

A happy horse

No access

Here are 10 poisonous plants to protect your horse from …

- **Privet** – luckily this shrub is rarely serious unless eaten in large quantities. The toxin glycoside ligustrin can cause diarrhoea and colic. Watch out for privet hedges bordering fields or people dumping their garden clippings.
- **Bracken** – the leaves and root of this plant contain thiaminase and are poisonous green or dried. Later symptoms include depression and rear leg weakness, coma and eventual death.
- **Acorn/oak leaves** – new leaves and green acorns are the most toxic as they contain a higher level of tannins (weak acids). If a horse eats large quantities, severe gastrointestinal, kidney and liver damage can occur, followed by death.
- **Potato** – research has shown that horses are more susceptible to potato poisoning than ruminants, even when non-green potatoes have been fed. Green parts of the plant are the most toxic, especially the skin of greened tubers.
- **Common ragwort** – the alkaloids in this bright yellow daisy-like weed cause staggering, loss of appetite and condition, straining to pass dung and gradual liver damage, usually fatal within a month. Small amounts eaten over a long time will have the same effect as one large dose, while the plant is more toxic and palatable in hay.

- **Yew** – this evergreen shrub or small tree is lethal even when eaten in small quantities – a horse ingesting just 0.05% of its bodyweight will die within five minutes. There's no effective treatment for acute yew poisoning.
- **Foxglove** – this plant with its characteristic pinkish-purple, white, yellow, or orange tubular flowers contains cardiac glycosides (including digitoxin and digoxin). Horses often die within 8–12 hours of consuming a lethal dose – usually in hay, although animals that have only ingested a small amount might recover in a few days following treatment.
- **Deadly nightshade** – when large quantities are consumed, this herbaceous plant can cause death from cardiac arrest.
- **Hemlock** – with its fern-like coarsely-toothed leaves and clusters of small white flowers in an umbrella shape, hemlock is easily confused with celery, wild parsnips, parsley, and carrots – but smells of mice. If a sufficient quantity has been consumed, death from respiratory failure occurs within two to three hours.
- **Laburnum** – this shrub or tree with its drooping chains of golden flowers in spring can cause death within a few hours of only a small amount being eaten. All parts of laburnum are highly poisonous, especially the seeds and bark, which contain the alkaloid cytisine.

Land laws

Don't overstock your land — aim for a minimum of one acre per horse, and for better and easier pasture management, use electric fencing to split larger fields into smaller areas that can be alternately grazed and then rested.

Rotate paddocks so each one is rested for three to four weeks, in order to give grass the chance to recover.

Getting to the grassroots

Consider grazing your horse with sheep in winter — these 'lawnmowers' are good for patting down softer land without causing damage but don't allow them to pull up the roots — and cattle, which like the longer grass that horses reject, in summer. If done properly, this can help improve your pasture and lower the worm burden.

New beginnings

Harrowing your pasture between late March and April when the ground starts to dry up will not only help level the rough areas but is an excellent way to spread grass seed, stimulate grass growth, remove moss and weeds, and spread droppings.

If the field is too large to remove droppings by hand, harrowing and resting the field will help reduce the risk of worm infestation. However, avoid harrowing wet areas as this will leave unsightly wheel-track marks and may stunt grass growth.

Rolling the field a couple of days later will level the uneven surface and pack down loose soil. It will also encourage any newly laid grass seed to germinate.

Quick tip

BORDER CONTROL

Ensure the fencing around your horse's field is no higher than his back – to discourage him from jumping out. Aim for a height of between 3ft 6ins and 4ft 6ins. The gap between the lowest rail and the ground should be a maximum of 1ft 6ins – otherwise he might try to get underneath.

Bright idea

Temporary electric fencing is versatile, easy to use and ideal for strip-grazing and sectioning off areas of land. However, it should be checked every day, as it can become loose in wet and windy weather.

Introduce horses to electric fencing gradually – it's best to erect it near a permanent fence at first before moving it further in. Make electric and wire fencing more visible by tying strips of coloured plastic to it at regular intervals.

When running an electric fence, use a leisure battery (designed for caravans or boats, which don't need a constant charge) as opposed to a car battery, designed to be charged constantly by the car's generator. This will maintain a charge for longer, plus the battery will have a longer life.

Keep batteries well ventilated, clear of naked flames and prevent sparks by disconnecting the charger from the mains power supply before removing the clips from the battery. Don't touch battery connections at the same time!

A close shave

If you plan to work your horse regularly in winter, his thick protective coat will need to be clipped so that he doesn't sweat too heavily, become uncomfortable and lose condition.

The more frequently your horse is ridden, the more hair should be removed – if he's just worked at weekends, a bib clip (see below) should suffice, while horses that are in full work and mainly stabled would probably require a hunter clip.

Choose from the following types of clip ...

- **Bib** – ideal for horses in light work; hair from just the lower part of the neck and under the belly is removed.
- **Trace** – suits horses that are worked several times a week; hair from the lower part of the neck and sides is clipped.
- **Irish/Chaser** – a variation of the above.
- **Blanket** – good for horses that are ridden every day; just the hair on the back and quarters is left.
- **Hunter** – virtually a full clip, with just hair on the legs and saddle area remaining.

It's a snip!

If your horse is prone to being a bit fresh and putting in the odd buck, consider giving him a blanket clip rather than a hunter or full clip.

Short-necked horses will gain a more swan-like appearance with a blanket clip sited further back than normal.

"I have a new horse. I get her to come to me from half a mile away. With just a simple call. That's because she knows that when she's with me, she's taken care of. She trusts me."

Russell Crowe

First things first

Before clipping, ensure your horse's coat is clean and well-brushed as matted hair will blunt the clipper blades more quickly. Check your clipper blades are sharp – blunt ones can leave lines or steps. Sharpened blades are better than new blades – ensure you have two pairs in the same condition or you'll end up with a two-tone horse!

Bandage or plait your horse's tail to ensure stray hairs don't get caught in the blades when you're clipping round his flanks.

Make your mark

For a slinky, even clip, it's best to mark lines on your horse's coat BEFORE switching on the clippers! Damp chalk is good for this, although it can rub off and can't be seen on greys, while many people prefer using home decorating masking tape. But make sure your horse stands squarely on a flat surface.

Ensure the lines are equal both sides by using a piece of baler twine as a template across your horse's withers.

Smooth operator

Use a light pressure with long strokes to avoid the coat appearing stripy.

Always clip in the opposite direction to the hair where it changes direction, such as under the gullet, on the stifle and around whorls.

chapter 3

Clip tips for equine first-timers

If your horse has never been clipped before, or is nervous of the clippers, run them over the back of your hand first so he gets used to the noise and vibration.

Acclimatise him further by taking the clippers into his box every day – switched on – without attempting to clip him. If this freaks him out, go back a step and just go in with them switched off and run them over his coat so he gets used to how they feel.

Plugging his ears with cotton wool or sewing sheepskin into the ears of a fly fringe will help to muffle the sound, while clipping in the stable may help too (remember to put a small amount of bedding down and throw it away afterwards as it will be full of hair and clipper oil). Alternatively, opt for a pair of low-vibration or battery-operated clippers or ones that have variable speeds.

Gradually build up clipping a nervous horse – just do the neck in two strokes to begin with. Move on to the shoulder and leave difficult or sensitive areas – such as the head – until last when hopefully the horse will be more accustomed to the experience.

Tie him up with calm horses and clip them first so he gets used to the noise and learns there's nothing to be worried about.

Under control

A humane twitch can be used with expert help if a horse is difficult or unpredictable, or sedation — under a vet's guidance — as a last resort.

When clipping ticklish or sensitive areas, such as the belly or around the genitals, ask an assistant to distract the horse with a carrot, pinch a fold of skin on his neck to relax him, or lift a foreleg to prevent him from kicking out.

It's best to leave hair on your horse's legs for protection. Follow the lines of the muscles and aim for an inverted V at the top of the foreleg while the clip should slope up towards the stifle on the hindleg. If your horse objects to a foreleg being clipped, ask a helper to pick up and hold the opposite foreleg. With a hindleg, the foreleg on the same side that's being clipped should be picked up and held. Clip an inverted V at the top of the tail, too.

Safe and sound

Always use a circuit breaker if opting for electrically-operated clippers.

Remember to wear rubber soled footwear and tie your hair back if it's long!

When clipping a difficult horse or if there's a chance the horse will kick, form a chest-high barrier between you by using a couple of bales of hay, straw, or shavings stacked on top of each other. This will limit the range of movement and absorb any impact.

When to clip

September is usually a good time if your horse has not been clipped during the summer. Some horses are clipped all year round if they are competing. Older horses are also clipped in summer as some do not lose their winter coat fully.

If you only clip your horse during winter, you should do the last clip of the year no later than the first couple of weeks in January when your horse will start to grow his new summer coat.

As snug as a bug!

When your clipped horse isn't being worked, remember to use a quilted rug in the stable and a waterproof rug such as a New Zealand outdoors, to compensate for the loss of his natural coat.

Check your horse's rug fits him snugly by ensuring that:

- The top lies two to four inches in front of the withers.
- It finishes just as the tail starts (unless it has a tail flap).
- The outside edge is well in front of the shoulder to allow for free movement.
- You can fit two hands' width between his chest and the front straps.
- The top front strap is in line with the point of the shoulder.
- You can't see your horse's belly when the rug is done up.

If New Zealand rug straps are clean, supple, and correctly-fitting but still tend to chafe, try slipping a length of bicycle inner tubing over them.

A happy horse

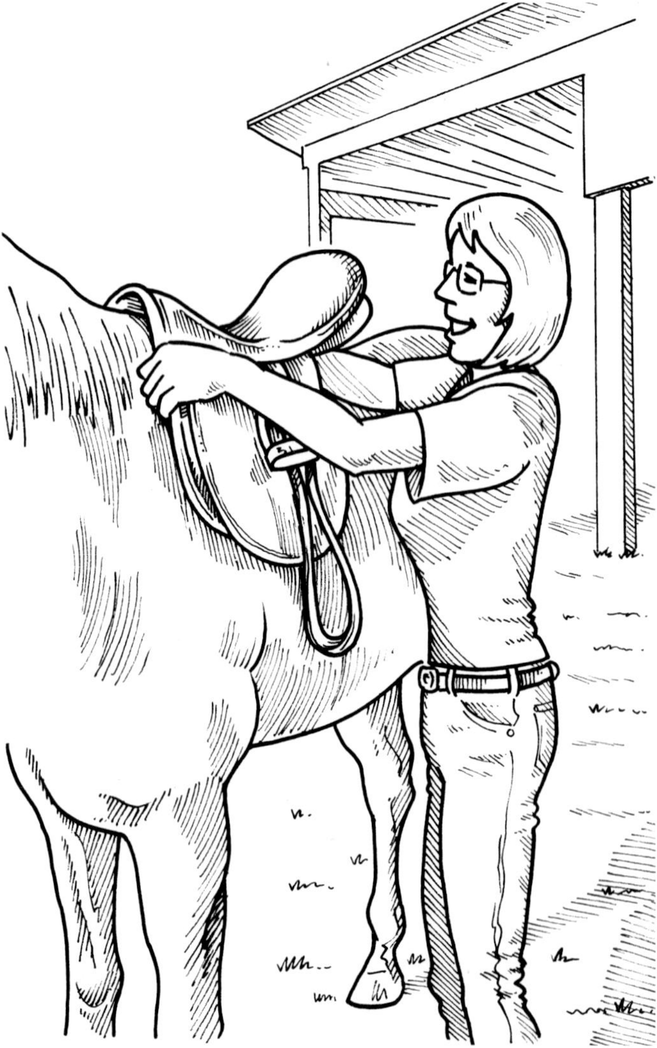

chapter 4
Saddle up!

Choosing the right tack and keeping it in good condition is vital in ensuring both you and your horse are comfortable while you're in the saddle.

There are different types of saddle to suit various activities (i.e. general purpose for all-round riding activities as well as specialist show jumping, dressage and Western saddles) plus hundreds of bits (from a simple jointed snaffle to a Dutch gag, for controlling strong horses across country more easily).

New saddles should be fitted by a qualified saddler and re-checked, ideally twice a year, while choosing a bit is best left in the hands of a knowledgeable person.

Girth reminders

For a girth to fit correctly, ensure there are at least two spare holes either side on the girth straps to allow for stretching leather.

After tightening the girth and before mounting, pull each foreleg forwards to iron out any wrinkled skin behind the elbow.

Slip the girth into a sheepskin sleeve if it is chafing your horse, more likely with youngsters or horses which are unfit or being brought back into work.

To wash non-leather girths (check the label first!), pop them in an old pillow case in the washing machine, so the buckles won't damage the drum.

Saddle checks

A badly-fitting saddle can cause discomfort and lead to behavioural problems. Watch out for:

- Uneven stirrup bars that aren't in a neutral position, are inset deeply, or are pointing inwards towards the horse.
- A gullet that's not at least three inches wide all the way along.
- Any lumps, bumps, or sharp points each side of the gullet, under the panels.
- Girth straps attached at an unequal distance from the knee rolls on both sides.
- A saddle that's too long – there should be at least six inches between the horse's loins (measure from the change in hair pattern at the horse's hips) and the rear of the saddle.
- A tree that's too wide – where the saddle sits too low and places pressure on the withers and spine – or too narrow – so it pinches the withers and spine. When the saddle has been correctly placed on the horse but not girthed up, you should be able to fit three fingers between the horse's withers and the pommel, and the flat of your hand between the front of the tree and the horse's shoulder, immediately behind his scapula, and slide your hand evenly from top to bottom. Tightness at the top or bottom indicates that the angle of the tree and angle of the horse's shoulder are not compatible. For horses with high withers, a saddle with a cut back pommel may give a better fit.

Salt water or surgical spirit can harden up skin around the saddle and girth area and help reduce sores and galls.

Bits 'n pieces

Ensure your horse's bridle fits correctly by slotting two fingers underneath the noseband (unless it's a crank-style noseband), a fist underneath the throatlash and two fingers underneath the cheekpieces.

Check your bit is the perfect fit for your horse's mouth by measuring 1cm ($5/8$") between the cheekpiece or ring, and the mouth. The bit should be high enough in the mouth to gently crinkle the corners – if it's too low it will bang against your horse's teeth. When looking for a new bit, use a saddler that runs a 'bit library' so you can try before you buy.

Sometimes a young horse can benefit from a smear of petroleum jelly on the outside of the corners of his mouth before the bit is put in, just to keep his skin supple and comfortable while he learns to take the bit.

Don't confuse the French link bit, which has a kidney-shaped central plate, with a Dr Bristol, which has a flat-sided one. The former minimises pressure and is a mild bit, while the latter applies pressure and is more severe.

Bitguards are rubber discs that are good for keeping a snaffle bit central in the horse's mouth but can be tricky to fit. Soak them in hot water first – to make them more malleable – and thread two pieces of baler twine through the disc. Ask a friend, or use a tack cleaning hook or door handle, to help you stretch it enough to fit the ring of the bit through.

With stirrup irons, they should be an inch wider than the broadest part of your foot, to ensure your feet don't get stuck.

Mentioning martingales ...

If your horse wears a standing martingale – which helps prevent him raising his head too high and beyond the point of control – check it's not fitted too tightly by pushing it up into his gullet. If it doesn't reach, it's too tight and will restrict his movement.

For more consistent control across country or when jumping, you could try adding an extra rubber stop to each rein to limit the movement of a running martingale.

> ### Quick tip
> **BOOTED UP!**
> To make it easier to pull on rubber overreach boots, soak them in hot water first. Smear a little Vaseline around the tops so they slide freely around the pastern without chafing the skin.
>
> Prevent your horse from getting brushing boot rubs – and stop the boots from slipping – by fitting an elastic cotton bandage underneath (such as a Tubigrip).

Numnah note

Sprinkle a little talcum powder on a natural sheepskin numnah before gently brushing it out to absorb sweat and dirt and help keep it clean.

Clean and sparkling

Tack must be cleaned regularly to keep it in tiptop condition and ensure dirt and grease don't irritate your horse. When cleaning saddlery, follow the grain of the leather, as this will help to retain its strength.

Save up all your ground down bits of saddle soap and heat in an old saucepan, together with some milk. Leave to cool before applying it to your leather tack to create a great shine.

Disguise any marks on your saddle by dampening them and rubbing with the back of a spoon in the direction of the grain. Also, gentle circular rubbing with a knot of horse hair will help reduce lines and marks caused by buckles.

To remove dirt from small and difficult areas of your tack, such as stirrup treads and the corners of your horse's bit, use an electric toothbrush (with a spare head, of course!).

Clean curb chains and bit rings – but not the mouthpiece – with metal polish, rinse and put them in your jeans pocket. The rubbing of your legs will soon shine them up!

If you've just bought new tack, wrap it in newspaper overnight when it has been oiled, to darken the leather and stop the oil evaporating.

When buying secondhand gear, ensure you clean it with an anti-bacterial wash before using it. Always disinfect mouldy tack as normal cleaning will not destroy the fungal spores, which can cause skin infections.

Breathe life into dry and brittle leather by applying warm oil. Apply a second coat a few days later.

Weather woes

If it starts to rain heavily while you're riding, resist the temptation to dry your saddle and bridle quickly with a hair drier or by using direct heat from a radiator. Leather that dries too quickly becomes cracked and brittle. Instead, wash off mud and dirt with warm water – never use hot water as leather will scald, just like our skin would. Then let your tack dry naturally in a room that's not damp or cold nor has the central heating on full blast. When most of the excess moisture has dried but the leather is still slightly damp, rub in some glycerine saddle soap. Once dry, use some oil or hide food sparingly.

In storage

Storing tack over the winter and want it to stay in tiptop condition until the spring? Bear in mind these three points ...

1. Use a leather food to prevent your leather drying out, otherwise it will peel and crack.

2. Store your tack at room temperature in dry conditions – leather stored in damp or humid conditions is more likely to become mouldy. Lofts or wine cellars are good places – less likely to suffer extremes of temperature.

3. It's a good idea to wrap leather items in a cotton sheet, pillowcase, or towel as cotton will absorb any moisture in the atmosphere before the leather can. Don't use polythene as any dampness will not be able to escape, which could encourage the leather to become mouldy. Some professional grooms cover leather tack in Vaseline before wrapping it in a linen sheet, to protect it from mould and discolouration during long-term storage.

All aboard!

If you're learning to ride, or returning to the saddle after a break, it's a good idea to book a series of lessons with a qualified riding instructor to get you off on the right foot and build confidence. In fact, even good riders benefit from the odd lesson occasionally.

On your marks …

After tightening the girth and running the irons down their leathers, ask a helper to hold your horse's head and the off-side (right) stirrup leather, to prevent the saddle from slipping, while you mount up.

Now, stand on the near (left) side of the horse, gather the reins and hold the pommel with your left hand. Face your horse's tail and turn the iron clockwise with your right hand. Place your left foot in the iron and grip the waist of the saddle with your right hand. Spring off the ground and straighten your left leg as you swing your right leg over the horse's back, taking care to clear the cantle of the saddle. Remember to move your right hand forward. Gently lower yourself into the saddle, gather your reins and turn the right iron clockwise before placing your foot in it.

Quick tip

GOING UP … ?
If you're not very mobile, or are a nervous rider, ask your instructor if you can climb aboard using a mounting block. Not only is this good for bad backs and stiff legs but it puts less strain on the saddle.

> **Quick tip**
>
> **DIGGING IN**
> When mounting from the ground, don't put too much of your foot in the iron as your toe will dig your horse in the ribs.

The long and short of it

If you're not sure whether your stirrups are the correct length, there are four simple ways to check:

1. Stand facing your horse's side and lift the flap of the saddle. Place your right index finger on the stirrup bar and, with your left hand, run the stirrup leather along the length of your outstretched arm. The bottom of the stirrup iron should just reach your armpit.

2. If the stirrup is higher than the top of your legs, you'll be putting excess strain on the saddle, your horse's spine, and your joints. Solution: find a horse with shorter legs, stand on higher ground, or let the stirrups down a few holes!

3. Once on board, let your legs dangle free down your horse's sides. The bottom of the stirrup iron should reach your ankle bone.

4. Position your legs correctly without the stirrups – if you have to drop your toes to reach the irons then your leathers are too long.

Remember to swap your stirrup leathers around as, over time, the nearside one will stretch if you mount from the ground, and your feet will be uneven in the irons.

chapter 4

Position pointers

When working on your posture in the saddle, think about recreating a standing up position while on board. There should be a vertical line from the shoulder, through your hip to your heel. Sit straight with your shoulders and hips square to your horse's shoulders. Reviewing your position with mirrors, your instructor, or a friend using a camcorder will help you identify any bad habits. Sit taller in the saddle by looking up and ahead. This will encourage your horse to look up, freeing his shoulder so his hind legs can come through and carry his weight better.

Visualisation can work wonders when you're riding. Imagine you are riding a tube of toothpaste, and you are trying to squeeze toothpaste from the back out through the nose.

Try some suppling exercises before climbing aboard: stretch your legs; lean backwards, forwards and to the sides; roll your head, neck and shoulders and swing your arms. Your posture will be better, you'll feel more relaxed and your horse will pick up on that. Allow your horse to stretch before working him too!

It may be a tough wake up call for your rear end but working your horse for short periods without stirrups will help strengthen your position in the saddle, improve your balance, and make you a more effective rider – honest!

A good exercise to help strengthen your leg position when you're not riding is to place the balls of your feet on the edge of a step, about two feet apart. Stay upright in your back and allow your heel joint to relax and drop. Bend your knees a little, and then work on stretching the back of your legs and keeping your balance. Or try walking slightly pigeon toed!

Hand signals

To obtain a light contact from the horse's mouth, your hands must remain still but flexible and follow the horse's movement. There must be a straight line from the horse's mouth to the rider's elbow. Hold your hands vertically with the thumbs on top, slightly above and just in front of the withers. Imagine you are carrying a tray with cups of tea, or that you are holding the bit in the horse's mouth without a bridle, using only the reins for control.

If you find you are constantly having to shorten your reins when you ride – perhaps because the horse is being lazy and not working from behind so is heavier on the hand – wind a plaiting band around each rein as a marker for where your hands should normally be. A simple and discreet tip!

Att-en-tion!

Getting your horse to halt squarely is an important part of performing a successful dressage test. If you find that one hind leg is further back, place your leg behind the girth on that side and nudge him forward. If it's a front leg that's at fault, nudging in front of the girth with your lower leg can remedy this. Always adjust the halt forwards, not backwards.

Quick tip

TROTTING ON
Steady trotting up hills and inclines is a great way of maintaining your horse's fitness levels.

Coordinating canter

Don't allow the reins to become slack when asking for canter as this will result in your horse running forwards in trot instead. Ask for canter while sitting up because tipping forwards will unbalance your horse and make it difficult for you to maintain the pace.

Cantering on a 'straight' circle, asking for an inside bend, will encourage your horse to take his weight on to his inside hind leg and create a more balanced pace.

Ask your horse to leg yield in canter from the track – this is a useful exercise to encourage him to work from the outside.

Ready for take off?

Do you have problems seeing a stride when jumping? Then a good exercise is to put a placing pole one of your horse's canter strides in front of the fence.

If you're in the habit of seeing a long stride and encouraging your horse to stand off his fences, try looking at the base of the fence rather than the top rail as you approach. Let the fence come to you, and it should help draw you closer into the fence.

For horses that rush their fences, go back to basics. Work your horse in trot around – but not over – poles on the ground, through wings and around markers, using lots of turns, circles and changes of direction. Then introduce one pole and trot over it, followed by three poles, before progressing to a small crosspole and finally an upright of the same height. Ask your horse to return to walk after each jump. This exercise should help temper both over-enthusiasm and greenness in a young horse.

Making strides

Schooling exercises are great for boosting balance, suppleness and accuracy – for you and your horse!

If you feel your horse tends to run on and get away from you, ride small circles to rebalance him.

Why not try schooling your horse one metre in from the outside track? You'll really have to concentrate but it's a great test of your outside rein and leg awareness and should improve straightness and security of the outline. Aim for straightness out of the corners and don't allow your horse to drift towards the fence or kicking boards.

A good suppling exercise is to ride three or four loop serpentines with a complete circle in the end of each loop before moving on to the next one.

When riding circles, maintain a consistent contact by resting your outside hand on the horse's withers, opening the inside rein so your hand is above the horse's shoulder and rotating your upper body to help turn the horse. If your circles tend to be more egg-shaped than round and your lines more wavy than straight, how about using flour and a tape measure to mark out an accurate circle or straight line in the school? Instead of drawing the whole circle, use dots instead.

Does your horse tilt his head while you're schooling him? Then try raising your inside hand for a brief moment, before returning it to the correct position. The more a horse leans, the lower your hands should be. If you find you are pulling against a forward-going horse, give with the inside rein to discourage him from fighting the contact.

Back to school

Once in a while, ask your instructor to ride your horse to refresh him, and also for you to see from the ground how your instructor asks for certain movements and how your horse responds. Ask friends and family to watch you ride, too. Even a non rider can often spot if parts of you are looking stiff or a little out of balance – sometimes they can notice a real improvement! Alternatively, ask them to video you so you can judge for yourself what you need to work on to execute that perfect turn or transition.

If you're schooling your horse after a hectic day and you're getting more and more wound up, take a deep breath and smile! Smiling helps to relax your mind and body.

Whatever your level, and whether you compete or ride for pleasure, learning from others can be really inspiring. So go along to a point-to-point, show, or event, or even hire an instructive DVD, to soak up some of the professionals' approaches and techniques – you're bound to be able to apply one or two!

Club together!

Why not dedicate a day at your yard or club to swapping mounts?

Experiencing a different horse's paces and movement can benefit both horse and rider, and gives you the opportunity to see how your own horse moves for someone else. Ask the horse's regular rider to critique or video you, and vice versa. Perhaps even perform a basic dressage test or jump a small course. Then compare notes afterwards over tea in the tack room!

Be prepared

You can never be too careful when hacking out, especially if you're on your own or riding a young horse. Always let someone know your intended route before leaving the yard. It makes sense to ensure the following items are packed in a bumbag around your waist or in a small backpack before setting off on a ride:

- Mobile phone (or some change to make a phone call in an emergency). Ensure you have stored the numbers of your yard and vet.
- Strand of baler twine (in case you need to tie up your horse).
- Card with the name and number of who to contact in an emergency, plus details of any allergies.
- Hoofpick (to extract stones from your horse's feet).
- Leadrope.
- Small basic equine and human first aid kits (if room).
- Ordnance Survey map, route, and compass (if going on a long ride).
- Fly repellent and sun tan lotion (if the weather's warm).
- Whistle.
- Bottle of water.

Time to reflect

Both you and your horse should wear reflective AND fluorescent clothing – including a 'slow down for horses' tabard – whatever the weather, as a bright sunny day can affect a driver's vision as much as bad light. Some riders believe pink, as opposed to yellow or orange, is a more visible colour.

If you can't avoid riding on the roads when the light fades, fit a safety lamp (white to the front, red to the rear) to the off-side stirrup.

In advance

As well as putting on your horse's headcollar under his bridle, it's a good idea to attach an identity tag with a contact telephone number on to your horse's saddle – just in case you part company when you're out riding.

Check your horse's shoes for looseness, and tune in to the weather reports before you leave – never set out if storms or thunder and lightning are forecast. Protect against flies and sun in the summer.

If your horse isn't keen to leave the yard, ride forward positively and firmly, ideally with a schoolmaster to give him security and confidence. Ask your horse to take the lead for short distances. Re-enforce your leg aids with your whip, then praise him and relax when he obeys. Using your voice will work wonders in encouraging and calming a nervous horse.

Saddle up!

En route

Observe the Countryside Code and always shut gates, ride round the edge of crops, and stay off public footpaths, pavements, and private land.

Remember that both walkers and cyclists, as well as horses, are allowed on bridleways, and riders can also use byways.

You can ride on verges providing there are no council signs prohibiting it. Keep an eye out for drainage ditches, rabbit holes, boggy ground, and discarded bottles and other rubbish which might startle your horse or cause injury.

When riding through wooded areas, look out for low-hanging branches and hidden tree roots and allow your horse to pick his own way through water.

If your local bridleway becomes dangerous or impassable — perhaps it is blocked by a tree, is water-logged, bordered by a bird scarer, or impeded by electric or barbed wire fencing — inform your local council's Rights of Way department.

Does your horse become over-excited out hacking? Exuberant horses often benefit from being turned out, schooled, or lunged before going out. If you school while out hacking, it will help to concentrate your horse's mind on work and not play. So your horse doesn't anticipate going faster, try to vary the spots where you canter, approach from another direction or go on an entirely different route altogether. Riding out with a bombproof horse might have a comfort blanket effect!

Safe not sorry

For safety's sake when riding on the roads, always familiarise yourself with the Highway Code and follow this advice:

1. When riding on a public highway, children under 14 must legally wear a hat that complies with current safety standards and is securely fastened. But it goes without saying that anyone riding a horse, whether it's hacking along a road or schooling in an enclosed area, should always wear a riding hat that conforms to the latest safety standards.

2. When leading a horse, keep him on your left.

3. Bear in mind that when riding on the roads, conditions and situations can change very quickly. Remember that plastic paint – used for white lines and zebra crossings – and worn, shiny patches on roads can be slippery, as are corners – so don't trot around them! Grit or dirt provides a safer footing.

Quick tip

THE END OF THE RIDE
On returning, don't just untack and leave your horse in his stable or chuck him in the field. Give him a rub down or hose him if he's hot and sweaty. Massage his back briskly to help restore circulation. And always ensure you offer him a drink of fresh water.

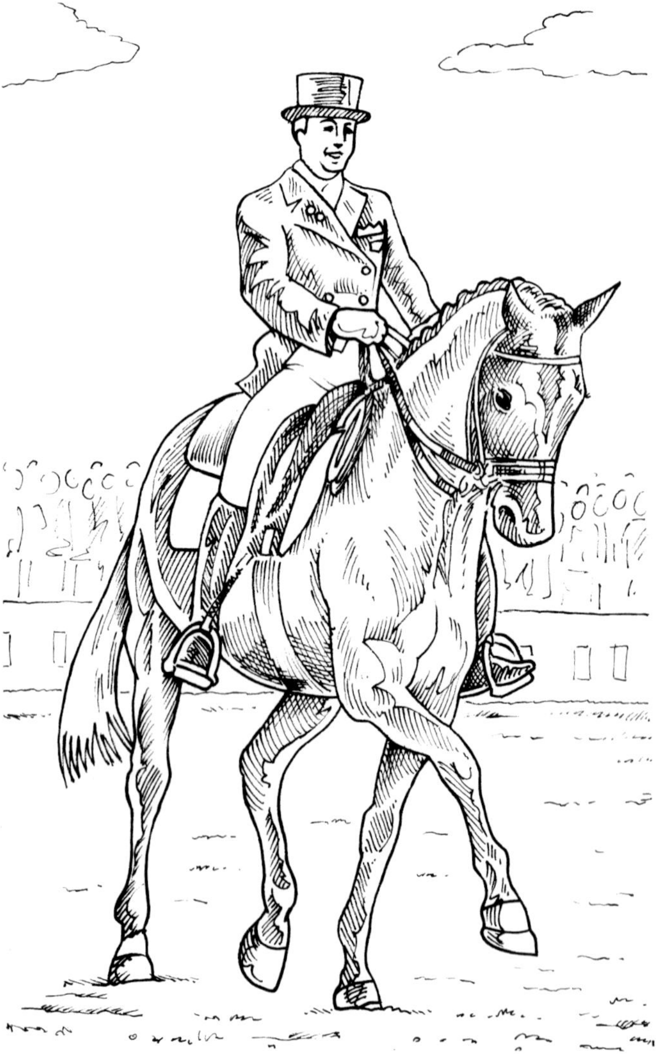

chapter 5
Show time

Showing can be great fun, providing you always put your horse's comfort first – if it's a hot day, stand him in the shade, and ensure he has access to water at all times. Remember – it's the taking part, not the winning that counts – you will always come home with the best horse, even if you're rosette-less!

Boxing clever

Always have your showing 'box of tricks' fully stocked and to hand at a show. Re-pack and check the contents the night before – it'll save you time on show mornings:

- Plaiting gear – needle and thread and/or rubber bands and scissors.
- First aid kit.
- Old track suit bottoms and T-shirt or overalls to keep your showing gear clean.
- Studs.
- Spare hairnet.
- Boot polish.
- Money for emergencies.
- A bottle of water to keep you hydrated.

> "There is something about jumping a horse over a fence, something that makes you feel good. Perhaps it's the risk, the gamble. In any event it's a thing I need."

William Faulkner

Wash and go!

Bathing, grooming, and plaiting are all necessary chores if you want your horse to look his best and impress the judges.

A few days before the show, bathe your horse with shampoo, not washing up liquid as it is too harsh, especially for greys and chestnuts which tend to have more sensitive skin. With a new shampoo, try it on a small patch on the neck and leave for 24 hours to ensure your horse isn't allergic to it. Remember to rinse shampoo out thoroughly as any residue can encourage dandruff and itching.

To remove the last residue of grease after bathing, put a double handful of soda crystals in half a bucket of warm water, wring out an old tea towel and rub it over your horse's body in sweeping circular strokes.

Bathing benefits

Bathing your horse can help to:

- Get rid of any loose hairs if he is changing his coat.
- Eradicate any parasites or skin complaints with the aid of a medical or herbal shampoo.
- Stimulate circulation and act as a form of massage.
- Make your horse feel and look good.
- Properly remove dulling grease and dust from the coat.

Choose a warm day to bathe your horse, and use a sweat sheet (a horsey string vest!) afterwards to help him dry off. But if you can at all avoid it, don't bathe your horse in winter as he'll need the natural oils in his coat for protection against the elements.

Prepare to plait!

Turnout for both horse and rider is very important, whatever the level of competition. So when it comes to plaiting manes and tails, practice definitely makes perfect.

Don't wash the mane and tail immediately before a show as this makes the hair too slippery to plait. A few days in advance, pull the mane so it's tidy and easier to plait. Pull hairs from underneath, especially if it tends to lie on the wrong side of the neck or stick up, to a length of 10–12 cms (4–5"). Pull the mane after exercise when your horse is still warm as the hairs will come out more easily while the pores are open.

Problems with a greasy mane and/or tail? Then dampen a clean cloth with surgical spirit or witch hazel and rub it over the hair.

Before plaiting, brush or comb the mane thoroughly then lay it with a damp brush to tame stray strands and hold the plaits in place while the hair dries (using sugar and water mixed together is said to help lay the mane flat). If dandruff is a problem, make sure you wet the mane more, so you can flick out any dry, scaly bits.

Divide the mane into equal sections, using rubber bands, and dampen again if necessary. Clothes pegs or bulldog clips are useful if you prefer to keep the rest of the mane out of the way while you plait. And remember to plait on the off-side (right) of your horse's neck — the side the judges will notice first!

Applying egg white, styling gel or setting lotion to the mane before plaiting is a cheap and easy way to stop split ends from sticking out and bind broken hairs, plus it makes it easier for you to keep the plaits tight.

Use a needle and cotton of a similar colour to your horse's mane, rather than rubber bands, to give a more professional appearance. It's perhaps a good idea not to use a needle and thread in the stable due to the lack of natural light and the fact you might drop the needle – bringing a whole new, relevant meaning to finding a needle in a haystack!

Don't be tempted to cut off wispy bits of hair afterwards – hairspray, mousse or gel is a much better taming tactic!

Some dressage riders prefer to use white tape around the plaits because they think it helps highlight the horse's top line and makes the neck stand out, especially if it's well-muscled.

Plaiting by numbers

Always aim for an odd number of plaits, excluding the forelock – seven for a pony; nine, 11 or 13 for a horse. If your horse has a short neck, you might find using 13 small plaits will give him a more swan-like appearance. Using fewer, larger plaits on a long-necked horse creates the opposite effect. Remember, though, that too many tiny plaits can look fussy while too few thick plaits may resemble a row of golf balls!

Another popular plaiting trick is to give a thin-necked horse a deeper, more muscled appearance by placing the plaits on the crest of the neck, rather than to the side. Thick necks benefit from the opposite treatment. For a tidier forelock, try putting it into a French plait instead of an ordinary one.

Protecting plaits

Even if it means an early start, always try to plait up on the morning of the show. Although you may think you're saving time the night before, you risk the plaits looking messy the following day and having to be re-done anyway. Also, leaving the plaits in overnight can pull the hair out and make the neck sore – not ideal if you want your horse to work loosely and comfortably in the ring. Leave his forelock to the last minute so he is less likely to rub it.

Keep a pair of old tights handy to protect plaits from hay and dust – secure over each one with an elastic/plaiting band.

If your horse has rubbed his plaits and split the hairs just before you go into the ring, undo the plait and apply a strong hair gel before re-plaiting.

Baby oil applied just before you go into the ring will make the plaits glisten.

To remove plaits afterwards, use a dressmaker's stitch unpicker as scissors can damage the hair.

Braid-me-beautiful

For breeds with long, flowing manes like Arabs and Andalusians or for horses with very thick manes, a decorative Spanish or running plait can help keep the mane both neat and attractive-looking. For a Spanish plait, part the mane down the centre so that an equal amount of hair falls down each side of the neck, and plait each side along the crest. A running plait uses a similar method but curves down and round instead.

A likely tail

As with the mane, your horse's tail should be pulled and washed a few days before plaiting – and the end trimmed too.

Before pulling the tail, ask someone to hold the horse's head and back him up to a closed stable door. Then you can stand on the other side without fear of getting kicked.

Wearing surgical gloves or a pair of lightweight rubber gloves when pulling your horse's tail will guard against blisters and give you a better grip on the hair. Pull your horse's tail from underneath at the top, working mainly to the sides, keeping both sides even. Only take a few hairs from the side each time as too many will make your centre plait look bulky.

Trim the tail so it hangs down to the point of the hock or slightly below when the horse is carrying it (10 cm/4" below the hock at rest). If your horse has straight hocks, a long tail can emphasise this weakness. Try shortening the tail to just below the hock's chestnut, in order to draw the judge's attention upwards to the point of his hock. For horses with poor hocks, allow a little more length for extra coverage.

Use clippers – instead of scissors – to give a cleaner line and smarter finish to the end of a tail.

Apply a tail bandage for short periods each day until the show, to help flatten the hair and train the shape of the tail.

Make a thin tail look wavy and full by plaiting it when it is still wet after washing. Unplait when it's dry, and comb through with your fingers, not a brush, which will break the hairs.

Show time

An all-round trim

Trimming your horse's legs and under his jaw with clippers helps give a neat outline – but if he is slightly light of bone, don't trim down the back of his legs as you'll accentuate this defect.

When trimming fetlocks and the hair around the coronet band, use scissors with rounded ends for a more professional – and safe – finish. Those trimming combs with a replaceable razor blade screwed in over the teeth (used by dog groomers) can be quite handy for this job as well.

Tidy traveller

If your horse is an inexperienced traveller, practise loading and unloading in the weeks and days leading up to the show. Drive round the block, slowly increasing the time he is on board.

For horses which tend to sweat up while travelling, use a cooler rug rather than a string-type sweat sheet as the former won't leave his coat imprinted with its pattern.

A pair of old tights will come in handy to use over a plaited tail, under a bandage, to protect your handiwork and keep it clean while en route. When taking the bandage off, remember to unwind rather than pull from the top!

Safe landing!

On arriving at the show, park in a shady area on level ground – take a block of wood in case you need to level up the ramp.

Having unloaded your horse, wipe metholated spirits over his body with a cloth to get rid of the dust from the journey and give his coat a professional shine.

If your horse is fussy and won't drink water away from home, either take supplies from the yard or try adding a little peppermint cordial to the water.

First show? The traditional way of warning fellow competitors that your horse is a novice is by tying a green ribbon round his tail. Similarly, a red ribbon signifies that your horse is known to kick.

Tack tips

Consider how your tack will suit your horse at a show: a fine head tends to look at its best in a thin, lightweight bridle while more workmanlike gear with a wider noseband would look better on a cob.

A straight-cut saddle will show off your horse's shoulder more – but make sure the seat is comfortable for both you and the judge! Remember that a high pommel, for instance, will not go down so well with a male judge, while a larger framed judge might not appreciate a tiny seat! If you're small-framed it might be worth using a saddle that's slightly too big for you (but still fits your horse well) so it's more likely to be comfortable for the judge – use bigger stirrup irons and longer leathers, too.

Avoid oversized or badly fitting numnahs as they can spoil the overall effect of your turnout. The professionals use pure sheepskin numnahs that fit the saddle exactly and do not move or slip.

Always introduce new pieces of tack – particularly bits – at home first.

If performing a dressage test, a hunting breastplate can give the impression that your horse has a rounder neck and can help break up big shoulders for horses who tend to go on to the forehand.

When using a double bridle (consisting of a curb – or Weymouth bit and a snaffle – bridoon), which is compulsory at advanced level dressage, ensure you twist the curb chain clockwise so that all the links are lying flat, before fastening it.

Then thread the thin leather lip strap (which is designed to keep the chain still) through a separate link in the middle of the chain and buckle on the nearside of the bit, in the metal loop above the bottom ring of the curb.

Tricks of the trade

Keep spent matchsticks handy for getting saddle soap out of the holes in stirrup leathers and other hard-to-reach places.

If you're using studs for extra grip in a competition, clean out the holes in your horse's shoes the night before with a horseshoe nail and pack them with cotton wool dipped in oil or Vaseline. This helps the cotton wool stay in place and keeps the holes rust-free. A pair of point-nosed tweezers will come in handy for pulling the cotton wool out. Not only will this routine save you time on the day – no scraping out dirt when you're in a hurry to load up – but will make fitting the studs easier.

Quick tip

BLEMISH BUSTERS!
Boot polish is the tried and tested old-fashioned way to hide blemishes (scars or white hairs) on a dark horse's coat; chalk or talcum powder for marks on a grey, and shoe whitener to brighten up socks. Plus there is now a bewildering choice of horsey makeup on the market for this specific purpose.

Dress to impress

Don't forget that the smallest detail can count and make all the difference.

Buying the best jacket you can afford will enhance your appearance no end. Try to match the colours of your show shirt and tie with your horse's browband.

Store your hat away from direct sunlight to prevent it fading – ideally in a purpose-made hat bag, while just before a show, hold a velvet-covered hat over the steam from a boiling kettle to raise the nap of the material and make it look like new. A suede shoe spray of the appropriate colour can help lift tired or worn velvet hats.

With rubber riding boots, use a little furniture polish from an aerosol for a dazzling shine.

For extra neatness, trim off the corners of your number. Rounded edges are also less likely to curl up.

Pop the flower for your button hole in some damp kitchen roll, wrapped with foil, in the fridge overnight to keep it fresh and prevent it from opening further.

Girls! Don't wear too much make-up for a showing class – less is more!

And never under-estimate the power of wearing a smile – whatever discipline you are doing – at least the judge will think you are enjoying yourself, which after all, is what it's all about!

Finishing touches

Bic razors are handy for removing the whiskers around your horse's muzzle – although some owners don't like doing this because horses use their whiskers to gauge distances. However, particularly for horses that lack breeding, removing the whiskers and adding a dash of baby oil to the muzzle, eye area, chestnuts, and under the tail, can inject a touch of class.

If applying coat gloss to give your horse that final overall shine, remember not to use it on the saddle area as it could cause the saddle to slip. Be warned that coat conditioner can make your reins slippery too!

Keep some Sellotape handy for removing hairs from your clothes and your horse's numnah.

Just before you jump on board, apply hoof oil so it looks fresh and you're less likely to mess up your clean show clothes. Even ensure the soles of your boots are clean!

In fact, it makes sense to wear an old pair of overalls or a tracksuit over your show clothes, which can be stripped off just before you climb on board and ride into the ring – thereby keeping any smears or stains to a minimum. That's unless you are lucky enough to have a groom or helper on hand to do all your dirty work, of course!

If you have a young horse who is bothered by the noise at competitions, cut down some sponges and insert the pieces in his ears.

Be nice!

Always be courteous to your fellow competitors and consider their needs as well as your own – don't hog the practice fence for longer than necessary and don't get too close to other riders' horses.

Why not offer to help higher or lower practice poles for your fellow competitors once you've finished in the ring? You never know when you might need their help in the future!

Keep your cool!

So you've got to the show and both you and your horse are looking your best. Now all you have to do is compete!

Sounds easy – unless you feel like you're having a panic attack! Nerves affect us all – even the top riders have butterflies and some adrenaline is a good thing. Breathing slowly and deeply can help slow your heart rate. Take a quiet moment to close your eyes and picture yourself performing a perfect dressage test or jumping a clear round – always expect the best, not fear the worst!

Quick tip
STAY CALM!
Does your horse fidget and refuse to stand quietly in line while the judges make their decision? Then distract him by scratching very hard just below his withers, or by pinching a fold of his skin.

In the clear

If you've entered a show jumping class, here are a few tips to help you remember the course and boost your confidence …

- Arrive early so you are not flustered from the start. Find a plan of the course and concentrate on walking the exact route you plan to take. Walk through the start – many riders don't do this – and look for your approach into the first fence, then the second, as you will need to be thinking about this as you land. After every three or four fences, stop and retrace your steps so they become entrenched in your mind.

- Walk the course at least twice, and ideally, have a more experienced rider with you. Don't be afraid to ask a professional if you can walk round with them – most are happy to share their expertise.

- With any tricky doubles, combinations, or related distances, stride them out and remember to walk through the finish.

- Talking yourself round the course – "one is the upright; two the parallel; three the rustic" etc – might also help you remember the route.

- If you have the luxury of being placed down the order, it will help to watch the first few riders' rounds to remind you of the route and to see if there are any bogey fences.

- Remember, if the show operates a flag system, red is on your right ("RR"!) and white is on your left!

- Note any areas where the ground is wet, muddy, or rough, so you can plan how to ride or avoid it.

Ways to warm up well

Start warming up your horse about 40 minutes before it's your turn in the ring – even longer if he's young. To begin with, walk your horse quietly to settle him, get him used to the surroundings and loosen his muscles.

Introduce trot and canter and do some suppling exercises such as leg yield and shoulder-in plus plenty of transitions. When your horse is ready, trot him over his first practice fence two or three times – a crosspole will encourage him to jump in the middle – before tackling a small upright in canter.

Start small and raise the fence gradually to build and keep both your own and your horse's confidence.

When you are happy with the way your horse is going, progress to jumping first an ascending spread, increasing the height and width each time, then a parallel. If things go wrong, simply put the poles down a couple of notches and start again. If all is going well, you probably won't need to jump your horse more than eight times before going into the ring.

It's best to have made a good job of your last practice jump. Always remember to ride away from the fence – as if you were approaching the next one – so your horse doesn't get into the habit of switching off every time he lands.

And the best tip? Think positively! Always tell yourself you're going to do well before entering the ring. If you think you'll have a fence down, you probably will!

> "When I'm approaching a water jump, with dozens of photographers waiting for me to fall in, and hundreds of spectators wondering what's going to happen next, the horse is just about the only one who doesn't know I am Royal!"

Princess Anne

Cross-country hang ups

Does your horse waver from water, dump you in ditches, baulk at banks or hurl you at hedges? Then only by practising the bogey fence at home will you overcome this particular hurdle – literally!

If your horse has a problem with water and your budget won't stretch to buying a water tray, improvise with blue plastic sheets laid on the ground. Concentrate on schooling your horse over a variety of home-made water-type obstacles in a balanced and forward canter. If necessary, follow an older, more experienced horse, that's not likely to spook.

Is there a ford or stream with a firm bottom within hacking distance? Then walk your horse quietly into it, ideally following a reliable schoolmaster. Once the horse becomes more confident, progress to trot.

With ditches, approach in walk and give your horse time to look – rather like jockeys do with the first fence at the Grand National! Use inviting tools such as wings or a single rail to help guide the horse over the obstacle. Alternatively, find a shallow depression in the ground or a drainage ditch and walk your horse over it. If this causes a problem, lead him over first then ask a helper to lead him over with you on board.

Go cross-country schooling or book yourself on a cross-country training clinic to introduce your horse to as wide a variety of fences as possible. Always aim to end the session on a good note.

And although it might be difficult at first, teach yourself not to concentrate on the problem fence – look over and away from it and think about the next obstacle.

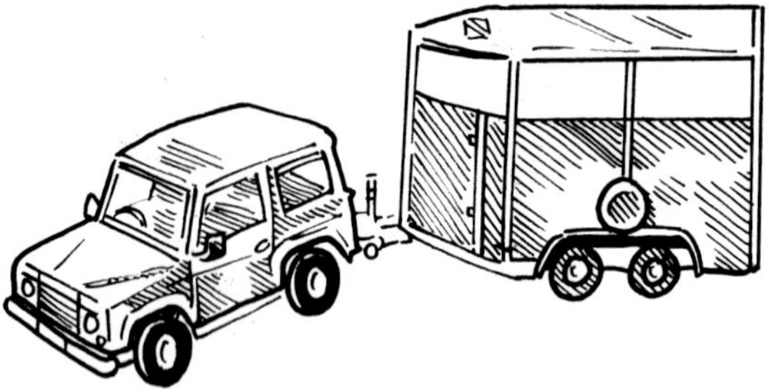

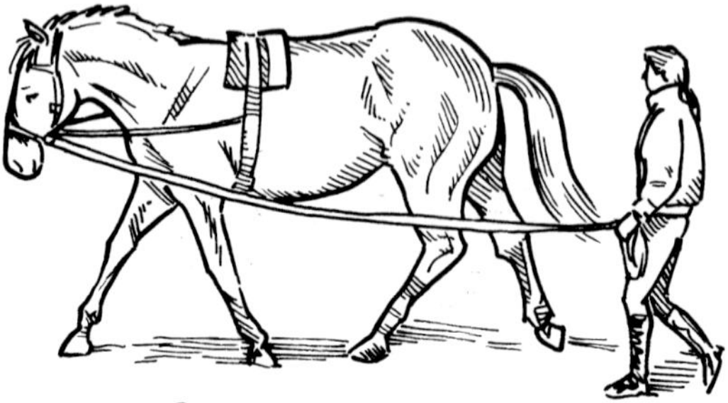

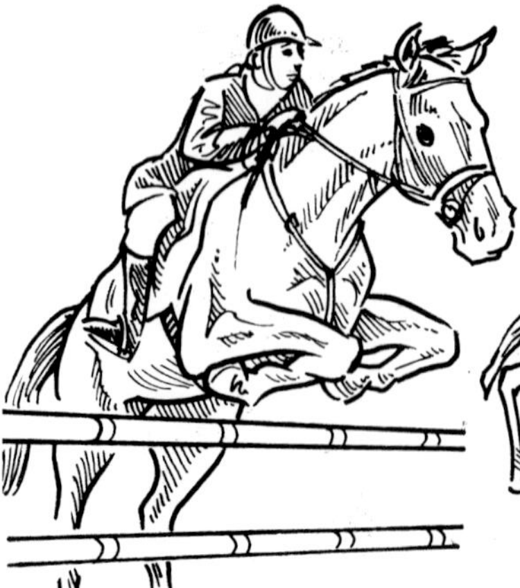

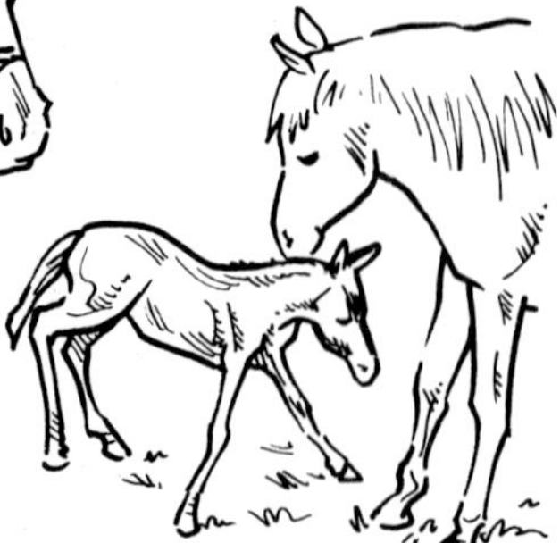

chapter 6
Tail end

Getting hitched

Towing a trailer or driving a lorry requires skill, awareness and confidence. If you're a trailer towing virgin, why not book yourself on to a specialist course? Various companies organise these – visit **www.learners.co.uk/towing** for more information.

If you passed your car driving test on or after 1st January 1997, you might need to pass a separate towing test to tow a trailer or caravan weighing more than 750kg MAM (Maximum Authorised Mass).

Speed control

When towing on single carriageway de-restricted roads, remember the maximum speed limit is 50mph, while on dual carriageways and motorways, the maximum limit is 60mph.

Courtesy cars!

The longer the distance you need to travel, the more chance a queue of slow moving traffic will build up behind you, especially if much of your route involves narrow roads or country lanes. Be considerate – pull over into a passing place or lay-by when it's safe to do so, to let cars pass you.

Get into gear

Before towing your horse, especially in winter, you'll need to plan well ahead. Don't forget:

- To fill up with fuel, and check oil, battery, and water levels, as well as tyre tread and pressure and brakes. Also top up your vehicle's windscreen washer and cooling system with anti-freeze, to avoid burst radiators, split hoses, and cracked engine blocks.
- To check your load distribution (aim for 50-75kg on the drawbar) and coupling height.
- To make sure lights, electrics and indicators are working; the trailer's jockey wheel or prop stand is fully wound up and secure; the correct number plate is fitted to the rear; the breakaway cable is connected and the trailer is safely coupled with everything inside properly secured.
- To ensure that the flooring is safe – look out for any signs of rotting or dampness underneath rubber mats.
- A torch with batteries that work, plus some spares.
- A charged mobile phone containing the numbers of your vet and yard.
- Extra food and water for both you and your horse, in case you get held up.
- A section of old carpet, stored in your lorry or boot of the car, to use under your vehicle's wheels should you get stuck in mud or snow.
- A warning triangle, in case you break down.
- Human and equine first aid kits.

- Rugs for your horse.
- All necessary documents, such as breakdown cover and contact number, and your horse's passport.
- Sunglasses – in case a rare ray of sunshine threatens to dazzle you!
- De-icer and windscreen scraper.
- A map and detailed directions so you're not so reliant on reading road signs in bad weather.
- A small fire extinguisher, kept in your car or lorry cab.

Going backwards

Learning to reverse is one of the trickiest aspects of towing, but with lots of practise in a flat empty field or car park, you'll soon master it. Start off slowly and steadily by reversing in a straight line before progressing to backing round a corner. You'll need to steer your vehicle in the opposite direction to what you would normally do.

Place your hand/hands at the bottom of the steering wheel, keep them there and do not move them at any cost. Looking behind you, move your hands in the same direction that you want the back corner of the trailer to turn. Start off slowly until you get the hang of it.

Putting out traffic cones in a field, or even better, a disused airfield, to replicate gateways and lanes will be less stressful and safer than practising on the public highway.

On the road

If travelling a single horse in a trailer, he should always stand on the off-side (driver's side) for a smoother ride and to counteract the camber of the road. If travelling one horse alone in a lorry, it's best if he stands as far forward as possible.

When towing, never descend a hill with the gearbox in neutral, as the vehicle will run away quickly, greatly increasing the risk of you losing control.

After travelling a few miles, stop somewhere safe. Walk round the trailer to see that everything is still OK – check the tyre pressure, ensure the coupling and safety chains are still fastened, the lights are working and that everything remains properly secured. If you're travelling a long distance, have a rest break every two to three hours to run through these points, check over your horse and offer him some water.

Always make a note of the height and weight of your lorry in case you encounter low bridges or ones with weight restrictions.

A head start

Before travelling your horse, he'll need to be kitted out in certain gear to help guard against bumps and knocks while he's in transit. One such item is a poll guard, to ensure the sensitive area between his ears is protected. Threading the headpiece of his headcollar through an old sponge will do this job just as effectively.

Going round in circles

Need to exercise your horse but don't have the time? Then lungeing – using a long rein from the ground – is ideal for helping to maintain your horse's fitness, as well as benefiting balance and rhythm, correcting bad habits, increasing suppleness, settling an over-fresh horse before he's ridden, and varying routine.

You can lunge in a bridle or headcollar but a lunge cavesson is best. Start with five minutes on each rein and build up to 20–30 minutes in total. This is the equivalent of schooling your horse for an hour.

Work your horse for a few minutes on each rein before adding side reins, attached to the saddle or a roller, to give him the chance to stretch and relax.

Quick tip

SPACE PLATFORM

If you don't have access to an arena or manege, lunge your horse using a flat corner of an empty field (at least 20m x 20m/65' x 65'), which is neither slippery nor hard and has good going. Enclose the open sides with poles, barrels or straw bales so that your horse is less likely to be distracted.

Tail end

Trouble shooting

Does your horse tend to turn in on the circle and face you? Then pointing the lunge whip at his shoulder and showing positive body language should help to discourage him from doing this.

If your horse won't slow down when you ask, try altering your body language. Simply turning your body slightly away from the horse and dropping your eyes can have the desired effect.

Banishing boredom

So your horse doesn't become bored on the lunge and to improve his balance, try introducing transitions, ever decreasing circles and extension and collection.

Vary the exercise further by adding poles – in a fan shape if you want him to tackle them on the circle or run alongside him in a straight line – to help boost his athleticism.

Pole position

When lungeing over poles, gauge your horse's stride and check distances by ensuring that his hind foot lands exactly half way between the poles. For a 12.2hh pony, the distance between each pole should be no less than 1.15m (3ft 9in); 1.25m (4ft) for a 14.2hh; 1.3m (4ft 6in) for a 15.2hh, and 1.5m (5ft) for a 16hh-plus.

Quick tip

OTHER EXERCISE ALTERNATIVES ...
Groundwork training such as leading your horse through a home-made obstacle course or long reining can also be useful ways of exercising your horse, especially in winter.

Crossing boundaries

Ladder reins are a really good teaching aid for both beginners and disabled riders, as the leather steps demonstrate how and where riders should hold the reins.

Rubber reins with coloured sections are not only good for teaching disabled riders and beginners where to hold the reins, but help those of us who confuse left with right! Different coloured gloves are also good for this.

Dressage

Not for nothing is the graceful and elegant art of dressage known as ballet on horseback. Whether you are riding at preliminary or grand prix level, always aim to achieve the following six goals in your training: suppleness, rhythm, contact, straightness, impulsion, and collection.

Wear dark rather than light-coloured gloves to deflect the judge's attention away from your hands.

Endurance

The equine equivalent of running a marathon, endurance or trail riding is reserved for those of us with stamina and resilient rear ends who love spending hours (and hours and hours … !) in the saddle.

If you want to have a go at a novice endurance event, ensure your horse is fit enough to take part first. As a rough guide, you need to build up to one hour's riding every day for five or six days a week over several weeks, to be able to cope with a 30 to 50 kms (20 to 30 mile) ride. Remember to increase the time gradually and make good use of any hills nearby to boost fitness levels.

Side-saddle

For hundreds of years, riding side-saddle was considered the only way for ladies to travel on horseback. Its popularity declined following the Second World War but has since been revived.

If you and your horse have reached a certain level in one discipline and are unlikely to progress further – or are just plain bored with riding astride – give the sport a go!

Because both of your legs are on the near (left) side of the horse, avoid bad habits like allowing your left heel to creep up. Sit still, straight and square, with your shoulders level and your right toe and left heel down.

Another tip is to try to keep your right thigh in contact with the saddle, thereby transferring your weight further forward – rising trot is a good exercise for this.

And if you feel brave enough to try jumping side-saddle, fold your body forward – rather than out of the saddle – as you go over the fence, moving towards your horse's right ear as this will counteract a natural tendency for you to be thrown to the left.

Driving

For those who prefer to follow a horse rather than be on one, driving is the ideal solution! However, a horse must always wear blinkers when he's being driven so he can't see the carriage following him and be distracted or spooked.

For safety's sake, always have someone holding the horse's head when you get in or out of the carriage, and never take a bridle off while the horse is still attached to the carriage.

Show jumping

Once mastered, show jumping is one of the most rewarding and satisfying equestrian sports: there are always bigger and trickier fences and combinations to tackle – in a time faster than anyone else. The bar is always being raised – literally!

If you're not used to riding with shorter stirrups, practise by leaning against a wall with your legs at right angles. It hurts, but it helps build up your leg muscles and strengthen them for the jumping position.

When learning to jump, your instructor will probably tell you to practise the jumping position – folding forwards from the hips with your bottom out of the saddle and the weight in your heels – in walk, trot and canter first, before progressing to tackling trotting poles and finally, a small crosspole. It takes budding show jumpers a while to learn how to spot a stride, but it comes with practise.

Eventing

Probably the most adrenaline-fuelled of all equestrian sports, riding cross-country requires high levels of skill, accuracy, and bravery.

When tackling any level of event, remember that changing light conditions can cause even straightforward obstacles to appear spooky to your horse, particularly when riding from light into shade. Sit up, encourage your horse onto as straight a line as possible and ride forward with plenty of impulsion – not speed as this will give your horse's eyes even less time to adjust.

Eventing tack tips

To prevent the saddle from slipping across country, sew a chamois leather to the numnah. And don't forget a breastplate!

Tie the headpiece of the bridle to the first plait, so if you fall off you won't take the bridle with you!

Exercising eventing caution

With a young horse, it might be better to trot, rather than canter, the last few strides into a water obstacle. Launching into it might frighten your horse and cause him to refuse next time.

Avoid picking up a tendon injury at the end of your round by not stopping suddenly at the finish. Either slow down gradually or ride a few circles to keep the momentum going.

Good breeding

The decision to breed from your horse must never be taken lightly as it requires a great deal of knowledge and experience. There is simply no point breeding from a horse with a poor temperament and/or conformation.

When looking for a stallion to cover your mare, avoid butch, oversized individuals to limit the risk of a coarse foal with a lack of agility. Look for an athletic, balanced stallion which moves well, has good carriage and a kind eye. His conformation should include short cannons and flat bones, well-formed feet, a good neck and head set on a fine throat, and good length in the quarters.

Foal's gold

So your mare has finally given birth and you're the proud owner of a bouncing filly or colt? The first few hours of a foal's life are critical. Check his navel often – it should be clean and healthy, while the cord should dry up and eventually drop off.

Colostrum, the first milk from the mare, is vital for the foal because the antibodies it contains kick-start his immune system. If he doesn't receive colostrum within the first 12-36 hours of life, he'll become weak and sickly and perhaps die. Keep a close eye on him during this time.

Mare and foal may look the picture of health and happiness now, but when should you start to think about weaning?

Start reducing the mare's concentrates when the foal is aged three months and grazing well, to help her milk dry up and encourage the foal to eat alternative feed more readily. Ensure you step up the foal's concentrates at the same time.

Wean the foal when he's at least six months old and is on grass, hay, and weaning nuts – his large intestine must be able to cope with fully digesting fibrous feed. Five days before and after weaning, introduce probiotics to the foal's diet to minimise stress and prevent scouring.

You can either wean slowly – taking the foal away from the mare for an increasing amount of time each day – or separate them and keep them apart so they can't see or hear each other. It will help if the foal has some company – ideally another foal, but otherwise any animal.

Give seaweed to both mare and foal as this is an excellent source of organic calcium.

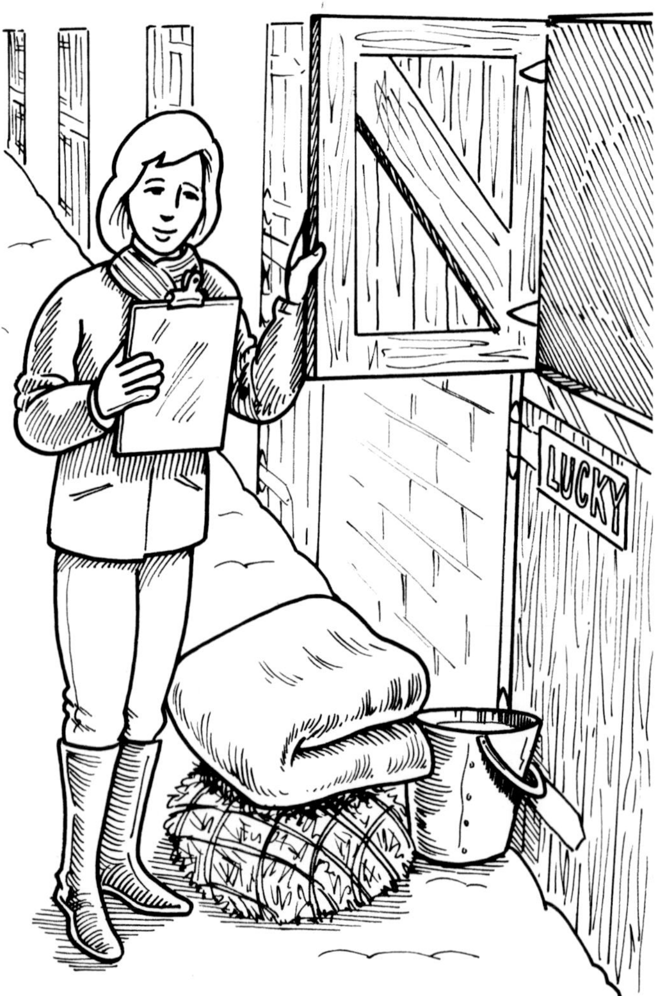
LUCKY

chapter 7
Against the clock

There's always so much to do and so little time when it comes to horses. Here are some time-saving tips to give you a head start ...

Pots of fun

Keep old supplement tubs handy and make up several days' worth of feed in one go, perhaps at the weekend or on your day off. Being late for work or school will soon be a thing of the past!

Hay fever!

Buy seven haynets – one for each day of the week – and fill them at the weekend or on your day off so that you can grab and run in the mornings. Store them in the feed room or hay barn, away from prying mouths.

Quick tip

PROTECTION RACKET
Use a cotton summer sheet under your horse's stable rug to protect it from grease and dirt – it's much easier to wash and dry than a thick quilted rug.

Super sacks!

Old builders' merchant sacks designed to hold sand or bricks are perfect for containing dirty bedding because they're strong, durable, hold twice as much as most wheelbarrows and are easy to wash and store. You can also carry your hay in one of these sacks to ensure it doesn't get blown around on a windy day and you have to spend extra time sweeping it all up!

Alternatively, push your wheelbarrow all the way into the stable, muck out, then place a sack over the top to stop bedding falling out or being blown around on your way to the muck heap.

Fashionably early

What a pair of old overalls lack in style they more than make up for in practicality – especially when you're rushing to get to work or the kids to school. Worn over your daytime clothes, they can make the difference between you dashing home to change and being late for work, or squashing your daytime clothes into a bag and looking creased and crumpled for that important boardroom meeting!

Machine clean

Investing in a webbing bridle for the winter can really cut down on tack cleaning. Simply wash it in the washing machine! But put it in an old pillow case first so that the buckles don't clank against the sides of the machine, or get stuck in the drum. You can wash fabric girths the same way – or alternatively, put an old sock on each end to protect both the buckles and your machine.

Quick tip

SHINE ON!
Running metal items like bits, spurs and irons through a dishwasher cycle will make them look like new!

Handy hint

Keep your hands clean and prevent sore, chapped skin and broken nails by storing a box of disposable gloves in the tack room. Wear a pair while mucking out or applying creams/lotions so you don't have to spend time washing your hands afterwards.

Powder power!

Shake some talcum powder into your horse's boots to keep his legs cleaner and drier, plus a puff of powder into your long boots will enable you to pull them on and off easier.

Getting the needle

When plaiting up for a show, thread several needles in advance and stick them into the front of your fleece so they're to hand and you don't lose them.

Against the clock

Winter warmers

Those long dark, cold winter nights don't mean you and your horse have to hibernate – thanks to a bit of forward planning and the following tips, you can keep both busy and sane ...

Spring into action

If you plan to compete your horse next year, winter is the time to expand your knowledge. The dark evenings are an ideal time to curl up on the sofa and study training videos or DVDs. Alternatively, check the Internet or your local riding schools/training establishments for any evening lecture demos, or devise a winter schooling plan with set training goals to keep both you and your horse motivated until spring.

> ### Quick tip
> **N'ICE IDEA**
> In snowy or icy weather, use Vaseline to grease the inside of your horse's hooves to prevent balling.

No sweat!

When returning from a wet, muddy, and cold ride, don't allow your sweaty horse to stand for long without a rug. Invest in either a wicking rug or a breathable cooler to dry him off and keep him warm.

Switched on

Always ensure you have a torch – and some spare batteries – handy when at the yard in poor light. Plus, you never know when there might be a power cut.

Chill out!

Sheepskin numnahs are useful for 'cold-backed' horses sensitive to chilly conditions.

Ground control

Putting down used bedding – shavings are particularly good – in saturated field gateways can help soak up some of the wet and prevent the ground becoming even muddier.

But for a more long-term solution, try laying bark chippings or some form of hardcore such as specialised plastic or rubber matting/chopped rubber or Tarmac scalpings (pieces of leftover crumbled road Tarmac) around the gate area. This might also help to prevent mud fever, especially if your horse and his field mates tend to loiter around the gate at feed time.

All wrapped up

During particularly cold spells, an old duvet is excellent used under a rug to add extra warmth without weight. In addition, they're easy to clean and don't harbour parasites. Also, if you have a thin-skinned horse that feels the cold more, don't underestimate the benefits of bandaging his legs at night.

Inside out

Soak hay in a shed or barn so it does not freeze.

Banding together

If your rugs don't already have them, put a rubber washer or a couple of plaiting bands around the T-clips, to keep them done up.

Age old problem

If you own an equine senior citizen, rug him up as soon as the weather starts to get nippy as veterans are more prone to losing condition in the cold. And allow him more time to warm up on cold mornings before asking him to work properly.

Cut and dried

Using a coat conditioner (not on the saddle area though!) will help mud slide off your horse, while applying a de-tangler lotion to your horse's tail will mean mud and muck are a lot easier to brush out, especially if you're in a rush or off to a competition.

Instead of washing off a muddy horse, especially in cold conditions, bandage straw around his legs and place a layer under a Thermatex or wicking rug, then brush off dried mud later.

Alternatively, paint liquid paraffin on your horse's legs before he's turned out so mud can be hosed or brushed off more easily when he's brought in.

And putting your horse's mane into long plaits will attract a lot less mud from the field.

Cough mixture

Does your horse tend to pick up a cough during the winter months? Then try mixing half a teaspoon of powdered mustard into each feed – an old wives' tale that some owners swear by!

Salt wash

If your yard uses road salt on concrete areas to keep ice at bay, remember to wash off your horses' hooves regularly as the salt will dry them out.

Harrowing salt into your outdoor school can prevent it from freezing over, plus don't forget to treat the steps and top surface of your mounting block, if you use one.

Alternatively, mucking out bedding straight onto the yard helps melt ice the natural way but remove droppings first!

Having a ball

To prevent water from completely icing over in freezing conditions, place a football or tennis ball in troughs and buckets. Keep a hammer handy in case you need to break the ice.

The heat is on

No heat in your tackroom to dry out wet outdoor rugs overnight? Then try draping rugs over a suspended or elevated jump pole or old broom handle, with the lining side uppermost, to prevent the weight of the water and mud draining through to the lining. Failing that, plait some baler twine and hang it across the tack room or drape rugs across a corner.

Freeze factors

Chain harrowing the surface of an outdoor arena just before a hard frost will prevent it from taking a hold. Remember that if trees overshadow your arena, rays from any winter sun will be unable to melt the frost evenly – so avoid those frozen areas.

Clear vision

If competing indoors in winter, remember to allow your horse's eyes time to adjust when going from dark areas outside into a brightly-lit arena.

Ski lift!

There are no prizes for looking glamorous or fashionable around the yard, particularly when temperatures plunge. For carrying out mundane yard duties such as mucking out or clipping, a pair of old ski salopettes — ask at your nearest ski hire shop for ex-rental ones — can be a godsend!

Looking on the outside?

Winter is often a good time to buy a horse because if you can cope with this time of year, the rest is a breeze!

If you're after a type better suited to living out in winter, then British or Irish native breeds (Highland, Connemara etc) and cobs are ideal because their chunkier bodies and shorter legs conserve heat better while their thick coats and long manes and tails have evolved to retain warmth. Plus their larger heads allow more space to warm the air as it is inhaled, and their small ears minimise heat loss.

Meanwhile, thinner-skinned, finer-coated, longer-eared Arabs and Thoroughbreds have evolved in hot, dry climates, and their bodies are better adapted to cooling them down rather than warming them up.

Quick tip
DOWN THE DRAIN!
Check and unblock the drains in your yard regularly as straw can clog them up and cause a flood during heavy rain.

Leap into action

Take advantage of winter to brush up on your own and your horse's techniques so you're in tiptop physical and mental shape come the spring. Use the time to focus on your long term aims, ensure the basics are secure, introduce new exercises and work on improving your position and your horse's outline and way of going.

Here are four suggested exercises ...

1. Smaller loops and circles to improve obedience, balance and suppleness – ride this exercise in walk, trot, sitting trot and canter, and with an advanced horse, you can introduce flying changes.
2. Serpentine loops of 3m or 5m (10′ or 15′) to aid suppleness – once you've mastered this, introduce some halt transitions over the centre line to vary the exercise.
3. Short diagonal lines – frequent changes of rein in walk or trot help develop flexibility.
4. Shortening and lengthening stride on 20m circles – ride in walk, trot and canter to help engage your horse and develop more scope in his paces.

Get packing!

If you're heading to an indoor show in winter, pack some snacks and hot drinks to keep your energy levels up, a warm jacket, spare socks, thick gloves, waterproofs, and a shovel and some old sacks in case you get bogged down in a muddy field. A handwarmer that you squeeze to activate – available from a saddler or Boots the Chemist – can be a lifesaver!

Lighter layer

Keep yourself warm by wearing a pair of tights – or silk gloves, socks and vest – underneath your normal riding clothes. A thin layer underneath is more insulating and less bulky than two thick layers.

Alternatively, a polythene food bag worn between two pairs of socks will also keep the cold out, especially if you're wearing rubber boots. And a cotton headscarf under your riding hat will help keep your ears warm – but you'll still be able to hear the traffic.

Quick tip

BUDGET BEATERS

If your budget allows, splash out on a synthetic saddle and bridle for use in the worst of the winter weather, thereby saving your more expensive leather tack for best – summer competitions!

Going barefoot

If your horse can look forward to a holiday in the field over winter, it might be worth having his hind shoes removed if he's out of work for a month or less. If he's not being ridden for a longer period, it's often more economical to have both front and hind shoes taken off.

Hot stuff!

While summer offers the best riding opportunities, the hot weather can have downsides. Here's my summer survival guide ...

Sense and sensitivity

Stock up on supplies of high protection factor sun cream if a period of hot weather is predicted – especially if you have a grey horse. Greys and horses with pink noses are more susceptible to sun burn.

Life's a beach

Lucky enough to live near the beach? Then take extra care with your tack after a ride as salt water dries up leather and rots stitching – rinse well with clean fresh water and leave to dry naturally.

Fly byes!

If flies bother you while you're riding, spray some equine fly repellent on your riding hat (see right for some suggested home-made remedies).

Buzz off!

Ward off those pesky summer insects with a home-made fly repellent that's just as effective as many expensive preparations available in saddleries and tack shops. Always try it on a small patch of skin first to check there's no adverse reaction to the mixture:

Concoction 1:

1 pint of cold stewed tea, 1 pint of vinegar, fresh garlic oil, several drops of lavender, tea tree, clove, and rosemary oils.

Concoction 2:

Mix a few drops of sandalwood and eucalyptus oils with liquid paraffin, liquid soap, and water.

Concoction 3:

A solution comprising two-parts lemon juice, four-parts vinegar, and four-parts cold tea.

Concoction 4:

Mix two tablespoons of meths, one tablespoon of washing up liquid, four tablespoons of vinegar and half a pint of strong tea – fill up with water to two litres and use as a spray.

Concoction 5:

Rinse the mane and tail with two tablespoons of cider vinegar to one litre/two pints of water.

Against the clock

Bug barriers

If flies are still getting under your horse's skin, try:

- Mixing garlic in his drinking water or feeding one clove of garlic a day to begin with, building it up to four or five daily – you'll find that this will ward off most insects (and everything else, come to that!).
- Siting muckheaps as far away from stables and grazing as possible, and removing droppings from stables and fields as often as you can.
- Providing a field shelter for your horse – he's more likely to use it in summer to avoid the flies than he is to get out of bad weather in winter.
- Putting up fly paper strips in stables, ensuring they're out of your horse's reach.
- Using a fly sheet or cotton summer sheet to keep your horse comfortable.
- Attaching a fly fringe to your horse's headcollar (either a leather or special safety one so it'll break/pull apart if it gets caught) or using a fly net/hood to cover his face.
- Applying a fine layer of oil such as Vaseline to the surface of your horse's skin twice daily, which will help prevent flies from landing and therefore feeding.
- Sponging your horse thoroughly after exercise so flies aren't attracted to his sweaty coat.

- Using an equine shampoo containing a mild antiseptic or insect repellent when bathing your horse.
- Avoiding areas where flies congregate, such as fields with droppings, water or woods, as well as dusk when there are more insects about.
- Attaching a few crushed stalks of elder to the browband of your horse's bridle while out riding.

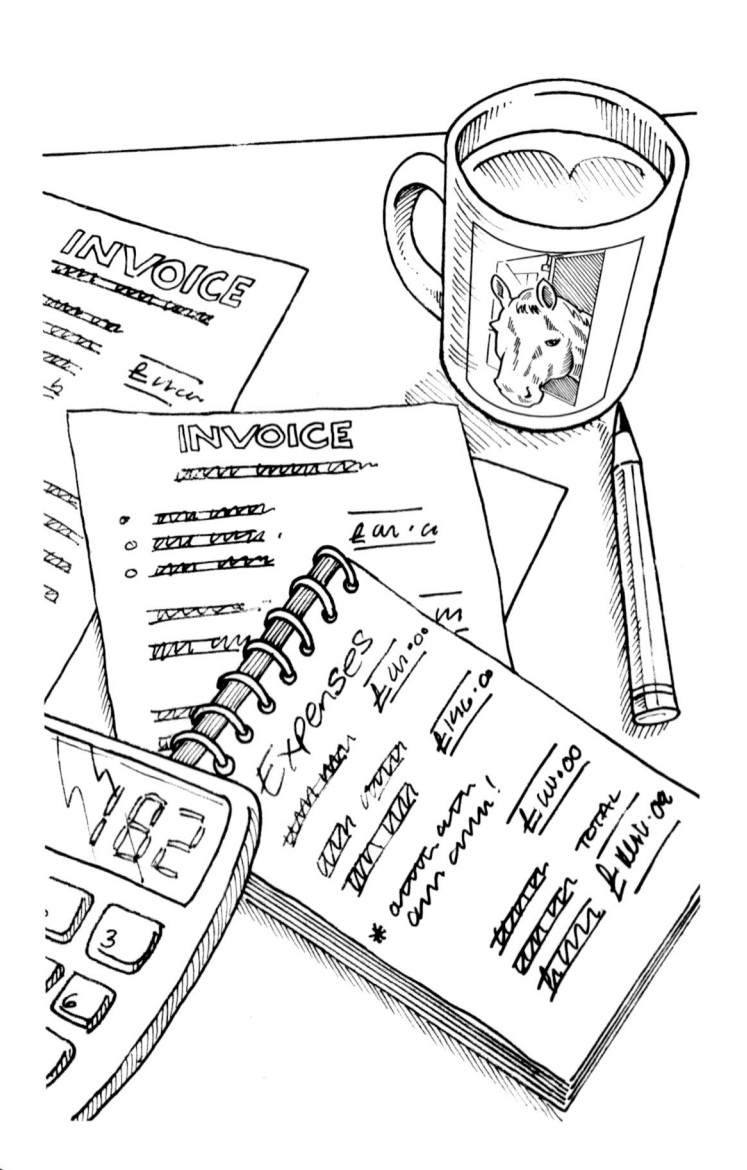

chapter 8

chapter 8
Money matters

Owning a horse is a big drain on anyone's bank account. Here are a few ways of cutting costs without cutting corners ...

Where there's muck...

Unwanted, old or damaged plastic washing baskets can come in useful as ideal 'muck lugs' or skeps for mucking out your horse – plus they are just a fraction of the price of these proper items to buy new.

Flawless flooring

Rubber matting can be a really good way of saving on bedding costs in the long run, especially if you stable your horse on shavings. Instead of using a bale of shavings every other day, rubber matting can help cut this down to around one bale per fortnight. Plus it helps cushion horses with sore joints and can speed up your daily chores – mucking out five stables can take just 25 minutes!

> ### Quick tip
> **IT'S A WRAP!**
> Old towels come in really useful for rubbing down your horse when he returns sweaty from a ride.

Smooth as silk

To prevent rug rubs, sew an old piece of silk or satin into the inside shoulders of your rugs, rather than buying more expensive purpose-made products.

> ### Quick tip
> **FOOD FOR THOUGHT**
> Plastic washing up bowls double as cheap and easy-to-clean feed buckets.

In the frame

A folding clothes horse is a great winter investment for your tack room – a cheap but practical boot drier.

Secondhand savings

Instead of discarding worn-out rugs, keep them to patch up future tears and holes, or for replacing or repairing buckles, straps, and fillet strings.

Added benefits

Sunflower oil from supermarkets is a cheap, long-lasting, slow-releasing supplement, high in protein. It keeps the gut moving and gives the coat a healthy shine.

Cod liver oil, which is good for condition and healthy joints, is cheaper when bought in a large gallon tin. Why not split the cost with a friend at the yard?

Keep in shape

Instead of throwing away old saddle soap tins, nail them to your tack room wall as bridle pegs. They're just the size to keep leather headpieces of bridles, headcollars and cavessons in shape and prevent cracking.

Take three...

... baked bean tins, remove the labels and ends from two (plus just one end from the third) and nail them to your tack room wall. Leave about four inches between each one and hey presto! Now you have a fantastic whip tidy for schooling and lunge whips.

Getting the boot

Keep your leather riding boots in tiptop condition by using large plastic soft drink bottles filled with water as cheap but effective boot trees.

Going green

Ask your local greengrocer if you can have – or buy cheaply – left-over succulents at the end of the day. Just check they are not mouldy before giving them to your horse though ...

Cost shavings!

Limit wastage when mucking out by sieving clean shavings through an old washing basket back on to the bed.

Money matters

In a scrape?

Hot day, sweaty horse? No sweat scraper? Improvise by using a double length of baler twine drawn across your horse's coat to remove excess moisture following exercise or a bath.

Group practice

Encourage everyone in your yard to club together and buy wormers in bulk, thus saving between five and 10 per cent – plus many companies offer free delivery with big orders.

Just bootiful!

If you can't afford a pair of new leather boots for the show ring, either buy secondhand or splash out on a top quality pair of rubber ones and ask a saddler to stitch garter straps on them for a professional look.

It's a scoop!

Cut diagonally across large plastic drink bottles to create home-made feed scoops.

D-I-Y waterproofing

If the seams of your New Zealand rugs leak during wet weather, rub candle wax along the stitching.

In the clear

Clear plastic duvet bags with a zip are ideal for storing rugs when they're not in use.

> "Whoever said money can't buy happiness didn't know where to buy a horse."

Anon

Pole work

Broken poles can be cut down and used as rails for stiles, or for marking out the edges of a schooling arena in a flat field.

All sewn up

Save the D-rings off old rugs or discarded items of tack and sew on to your New Zealand rug as a neck cover attachment. That way you won't need to go to the expense of buying a brand new rug and matching neck cover in one. Neck covers are great in winter for keeping horses warm and clean – and saving you grooming time.

Fishing around!

Mend your rugs using nylon fishing line or dental floss – strong, durable and waterproof!

Hand wash!

Wash your horse's rugs yourself in a dustbin or your bath, using hypo-allergenic washing liquid and a pole!

With New Zealand rugs, hang them over a gate and use a pressure washer to blast off all traces of mud and muck.

Cold case

Old chest freezers make great rodent-proof feed bins or storage containers for gear you want to keep clean and dry. For safety, disable the locking mechanism first, though.

Treading the boards

For a home-made portable mounting block, nail a flat sheet of wood onto the bottom of an old milk crate, to make it safe and sturdier.

Sleeping partner

Turn an old sleeping bag into a warm quilted stable rug by removing the zip, cutting out a semi-circular section at one end for the neck and shoulders and stitching around the edges. Strips of broad Velcro make excellent breast straps.

Shopping around

Top quality show jackets, boys' shirts and colourful ties can be bought for the show ring from charity shops at a fraction of the price.

Quick tip

PEDAL POWER

Bicycle puncture repair kits can be used for mending holes in rubber riding boots. The job won't look pretty but at least you won't have to shell out on a new pair and your feet will stay dry!

Disclaimer
The websites, services and resources listed in this book have not paid for their entries – they are included as a guideline only and the author/publisher does not endorse their products or services.

My tips

Index

A
Acorn leaves, 66
Allergies, 20
Allergy, dust, 59
Anaemia, 57
Andalusian, 24
Arab, 24
Auction, 11, 19

B
Bandages, 58, 60
Bandaging, 58, 60, 133
Bathing, 97
Barging, 31
Bed, 32
Bedding, 32, 145
Birth, 127
Bit, 79
Bit guard, 79
Blemishes, covering, 105
Body brush, 36
Boots, 147, 148
Boots, overreach, 80
Boots, repairing rubber, 151
Boredom, 29-30, 120
Box rest, 29
Box walker, 17

Bracken, 66
Breast bar, 31
Breathing problems, 29, 32, 50
Breeder, 11
Breeding, 126-127
Breeds, 24-25
Bridle, 79
British Equestrian Directory, 11
Brushing, 36-37
Bugs, 140-143
Buying a horse, 9-19
Buying, checks before, 14
Buying questions, 13, 16, 20

C
Canter, 17, 87
Cantering, 87
Catching your horse, 64
Charities, 11
Clip, types of, 70
Clipping, 70-75
Clothing, reflective, 91
Clothing, show, 106, 107

Clothing, winter, 133, 137, 139
Coat conditioner, 134
Cod liver oil, 45, 146
Cold spells, 133
Confirmation, vendor, 18
Connemara, 24
Cough, winter, 135
Countryside Code, 92
Crib biting, 17, 31
Cross-country, 112-113
Curry comb, 36

D
Dandy brush, 36
Deadly nightshade, 67
Dealer, 27
Dealer's yard, 11
Dehydration, 57
Dental hygiene, 61
Dentist, equine, 61
Diet, 45-49
Dressage, 104, 122
Driving, 124
Dust allergy, 59
Dutch Warmblood, 24

E

Eating, fussy, 48
Electric fencing, 69
Endurance, 122
Eventing, 125
Exercise, 20, 138

F

Feed, 20, 45-49
Feed scoop, homemade, 148
Feeding, 45-49, 129
Feeding, rules, 46
Fencing, electric, 69
Fencing, paddock, 69
First aid kit, 54
Five-stage vetting, 19
Flies, 140-143
Fly repellent, 141-143
Foal, 127
Fork, four-tined, 33
Forking, 33
Foxglove, 67
Freeze marking, 41

G

Gateways, field, 133
Girth, 77, 78
Grazing, 68
Grooming, 36-39
Grooming kit, 36-37, 39
Group practice, 148
Gums, 51

H

Habits, 20
Hacking out, 90-93
Hacking out kit, 90
Hacking out, preparation, 90-91
Halting, 86
Hand signals, 86
Hanoverian, 25
Harrowing, 68, 135, 136
Haynet, height of, 47
Health check, 19, 51
Heartbeat, 52
Hemlock, 67
Herbs, 50
Highway Code, 93
Home, new, 21
Homeopathic vet, 50
Hoof brush, 37
Hoof oil, 37
Hoof pick, 36
Hoof problems, 29
Horsewatch co-ordinator, 43

I

Icy conditions, 135
Identity chipping, 41
Immune system, 50
Inhalation therapy, 59
Insect prevention, 141-143
Insects, 140-143
Instructor, riding, 12, 15, 83, 89
Irish Draught, 25

J

Jumping, 87, 109-110

K

Kickboards, 35

L

Laburnum, 67
Ladder reins, 121
Lameness, 17
Leasing a horse, 23
Leg shape, 51
Legs, trimming of, 102
Lessons, riding, 83
Livery, 9, 10

Livery costs, 23
Loan agreement, 22
Loaning a horse, 22-23
Long back, 17
Lungeing, 119-120

M

Mane comb, 37
Martingale, 80
Money-saving tips, 145-151
Mounting, 84
Mounting block, homemade, 151
Muck heap, 33, 35
Mucking out, 29, 32-33, 130, 145, 147
Mucking out, clothing for, 130, 137
Mud, 60
Mud fever, 60

N

Neck, short, 17
Neck cover, 152
New home, 21
Numnah, 80, 133

O

Oak leaves, 66

P

Paddock fencing, 69
Paddock safety, 65
Paddock size, 68
Pasterns, upright, 17
Photographs, security, 43
Plaiting, 98-100
Planning permission, 35
Poisonous plants 66-67
Postcode branding, 41
Privet, 66
Property protection, 42
Pulse, 52

Q

Quarter Horse, 25

R

Ragwort, 66
Recurrent Airway Obstruction (RAO), 59
Reins, ladder, 121
Reins, rubber, 121
Respiration rate, 52
Respiratory problems, 29, 32, 50

Riding instructor, 12, 15, 89
Rolling, 68
Rubber reins, 121
Rug rubs, 146
Rug, waterproof, 75
Rugs, washing, 150

S

Saddle, 77-78
Saddle, fitting, 77
Saddle, straight-cut, 104
Saddle, synthetic, 139
Saddle position, 85
Saddle drying, 82
Saddle lock, 40
Saddle soap tins, used, 147
Saddling, 77-78
Sale of Goods Act 1979, 18
Sales agreement, 27
Salt water, 140
Schooling, 88-89, 112-113
Scraping, 31
Security, 40-43
Security, lorry, 42
Security, trailer, 42

Security marking, 40
Selling a horse, 26-27
Shetland, 25
Shire, 25
Shoes, 62
Show clothing, 106,107
Show jumping, 109-110, 124
Show nerves, 108
Showing, 95-110
Showing in winter, 138
Shows, travelling to, 102-103
Side-saddle, 123
Signals, hand
Sponges, 36
Stables, building, 35
Stable rubber, 37
Stabling, 29-43
Stirrup adjustment, 84
Stirrup irons, 79
Stirrups, 84
Stolen Horse Register, 41
Studs, 105
Sun cream, 140
Sunflower oil, 146

Swapping mounts, 89
Sweat scraper, 36, 148
Sweating, 132, 148

T

Tack, 20, 77-84
Tack, storing, 82
Tack cleaning, 81, 130, 131
Tack for a show, 104-105
Tail, washing & trimming of, 101
Temperature, adult horse, 51
Test ride, 12, 15
Thoroughbred, 25
Thrush, 29, 32
Topline, 17
Torch, 133
Towing, 115-118
Towing checklist, 116-117
Toys, 30
Trailer towing, 115-118
Training, 132
Trial period, 27

Trial period agreement, 27
Trotting on, 86

V

Vendor confirmation, 18
Vet, 19
Vet, homeopathic, 50

W

Warming up, 110
Water brush, 36
Water therapy, 63
Weaning, 127
Weight loss, 49
Whip tidy, 147
Winter, 130, 132-139
Wounds, 56-58
Worming, 20, 61

Y

Yard duties, 23
Yard knife, 33
Yard tools, 33
Yew, 67

Index 157

'The Greatest Tips in the World' books

Baby & Toddler Tips
by Vicky Burford
ISBN 978-1-905151-70-7

Barbeque Tips
by Raymond van Rijk
ISBN 978-1-905151-68-4

Cat Tips by Joe Inglis
ISBN 978-1-905151-66-0

Cookery Tips
by Peter Osborne
ISBN 978-1-905151-64-6

Cricketing Tips
by R. Rotherham & G. Clifford
ISBN 978-1-905151-18-9

DIY Tips
by Chris Jones & Brian Lee
ISBN 978-1-905151-62-2

Dog Tips by Joe Inglis
ISBN 978-1-905151-67-7

Etiquette & Dining Tips
by Prof. R. Rotherham
ISBN 978-1-905151-21-9

Freelance Writing Tips
by Linda Jones
ISBN 978-1-905151-17-2

Gardening Tips
by Steve Brookes
ISBN 978-1-905151-60-8

Genealogy Tips
by M. Vincent-Northam
ISBN 978-1-905151-72-1

Golfing Tips
by John Cook
ISBN 978-1-905151-63-9

Horse & Pony Tips
by Joanne Bednall
ISBN 978-1-905151-19-6

Household Tips
by Vicky Burford
ISBN 978-1-905151-61-5

Personal Success Tips
by Brian Larcher
ISBN 978-1-905151-71-4

Podcasting Tips
by Malcolm Boyden
ISBN 978-1-905151-75-2

Property Developing Tips
by F. Morgan & P Morgan
ISBN 978-1-905151-69-1

Retirement Tips
by Tony Rossiter
ISBN 978-1-905151-28-8

Sex Tips
by Julie Peasgood
ISBN 978-1-905151-74-5

Travel Tips
by Simon Worsfold
ISBN 978-1-905151-73-8

Yoga Tips
by D. Gellineau & D. Robson
ISBN 978-1-905151-65-3

Pet Recipe books

The Greatest Feline Feasts in the World by Joe Inglis
ISBN 978-1-905151-50-9

The Greatest Doggie Dinners in the World by Joe Inglis
ISBN 978-1-905151-51-6

'The Greatest in the World' DVDs

The Greatest in the World – Gardening Tips
presented by Steve Brookes

The Greatest in the World – Yoga Tips
presented by David Gellineau and David Robson

The Greatest in the World – Cat & Kitten Tips
presented by Joe Inglis

The Greatest in the World – Dog & Puppy Tips
presented by Joe Inglis

For more information about currently available
and forthcoming book and DVD titles please visit:

www.thegreatestintheworld.com

or write to:

The Greatest in the World Ltd
PO Box 3182
Stratford-upon-Avon
Warwickshire CV37 7XW
United Kingdom

Tel / Fax: +44(0)1789 299616
Email: info@thegreatestintheworld.com

The author

After starting out reporting for local newspapers, Joanne Bednall has spent 12 years as a staff writer on equestrian magazines, ranging from popular teen title Horse and Pony to adult monthly Horse, as well as penning several children's books on riding and pony care for Dorling Kindersley's Funfax series.

When Joanne isn't contributing to women's weeklies and specialist magazines such as Your Dog, she enjoys long country walks near her Staffordshire home with her Golden Retrievers, Rolo and Indi, and riding her thoroughbred mare, Antonia.

Thanks everyone!

Joanne would like to thank the following people for their help, time, support and/or input:

Adrian Milledge | Jenny Millman BHSAI Int SM | Amanda McGinnigle BHSII | Tara May | Michaela Twite | Gartmore Riding School, Hammerwich, Staffordshire | Liz Abbiss | Emma Butler | Claire O'Halloran